What the Experts Are Saying . . .

"Val Walker's newest book *Healing Through Wonder* is a powerful work—urging readers to draw upon their own resilience, particularly a sense of wonder as they cope with loss. Walker reminds us to embrace our own inner strengths as we struggle with grief. This book is a gift to anyone who is bereaved."—**Kenneth J. Doka**, PhD, Senior Vice President for Grief Programs, The Hospice Foundation of America, and author of *Disenfranchised Grief, Grief Is a Journey,* and *When We Die*

"Val Walker's profound journey through trauma and spiritual exploration is both heart-wrenching and inspiring. This book beautifully captures the resilience of the human spirit and the transformative power of connection and awe. A must-read for anyone seeking healing and understanding."—**Shari Botwin**, LCSW, keynote speaker, media contributor, and author of *Thriving After Trauma* and *Stolen Childhoods*

"*Healing Through Wonder* is a luminous testament to the transformative power of awe. Blending personal vulnerability with compelling research, this book invites readers into a journey where wonder becomes a profound source of healing and hope after trauma and loss."—**Scott T. Allison**, PhD, Professor Emeritus of Psychology, University of Richmond, editor of *Heroism Science* and *The Encyclopedia of Heroism Studies*, and author of *Reel Heroes, Heroic Humanity,* and *Handbook of Heroism*

"Walker's personal experience with trauma is both moving and beautifully written. Her study of awe as a source of healing for herself and others will bring hope, help, and pave a better future for many."—**Kelsey Crowe**, PhD, co-author of *There Is No Good Card for This* and founder of Empathy Bootcamp

"In the midst of illness, trauma, and loss, it is easy to feel alone and stuck in darkness. By providing a platform for the sharing of awe-inspiring moments, the Healing Through Wonder project propels us toward health by reminding us to step outside of ourselves and to celebrate our collective humanity and the wonder of the world."—**Annie Brewster**, MD, Executive Director and founder of The Health Story Collaborative, Associate Professor at Harvard Medical School, and author of *The Healing Power of Storytelling*

"*Healing Through Wonder* honors the truth that grief is not something to fix, but something to live within—and that awe and wonder can create space for healing without forcing it. Val Walker captures how openness and connection can gently accompany the grieving process, especially through the voices of those who have lived it."—**Glen Lord**, CEO of Peer Support Community Partners, Massachusetts

"Val Walker is gracious enough to open up about her own experiences and show us that the space that exists between trauma and self-compassion has the potential to make us feel comfortable in who we are and how far we have come."—**Lindsay Weisner**,

PsyD, co-author of *Ten Steps to Finding Happy* and author of *Psychology Today* blog "The Venn Diagram Life"

"In a world that often demands neat answers and swift resolutions, *Healing Through Wonder* offers something profoundly different: a compassionate embrace of mystery, awe, and the slow unfolding of healing. Val Walker's exquisite blend of personal memoir, neuroscience, and community stories honors trauma and grief not as brokenness to be 'fixed' but as wounds that call for gentle reverence and presence. This book reminds us that the path to wholeness needs courage but also moments of breathless wonder—moments that open us to life's beauty and connection."—**Antonieta Contreras**, author of *How Deep Is the Wound?* and *Traumatization and Its Aftermath*, blogger for *Psychology Today*

HEALING THROUGH WONDER

How Awe Restores Us After Trauma and Loss

VAL WALKER

BLOOMSBURY ACADEMIC
NEW YORK · LONDON · OXFORD · NEW DELHI · SYDNEY

Bloomsbury Publishing Inc, 1359 Broadway, New York, NY 10018, USA
Bloomsbury Publishing Plc, 50 Bedford Square, London, WC1B 3DP, UK
Bloomsbury Publishing Ireland, 29 Earlsfort Terrace, Dublin 2, D02 AY28, Ireland

BLOOMSBURY, BLOOMSBURY ACADEMIC and the Diana logo are trademarks of Bloomsbury Publishing Plc

First published in the United States of America 2026

Copyright © Val Walker, 2026

For legal purposes the Acknowledgments on p. 231 constitute an extension of this copyright page.

Cover design: © Diana Nuhn

Cover image © Getty/Vicki Jauron, Babylon and Beyond Photography

Author photo by Carrington Crothers

All rights reserved. No part of this publication may be: i) reproduced or transmitted in any form, electronic or mechanical, including photocopying, recording or by means of any information storage or retrieval system without prior permission in writing from the publishers; or ii) used or reproduced in any way for the training, development or operation of artificial intelligence (AI) technologies, including generative AI technologies. The rights holders expressly reserve this publication from the text and data mining exception as per Article 4(3) of the Digital Single Market Directive (EU) 2019/790.

Bloomsbury Publishing Inc does not have any control over, or responsibility for, any third-party websites referred to or in this book. All internet addresses given in this book were correct at the time of going to press. The author and publisher regret any inconvenience caused if addresses have changed or sites have ceased to exist, but can accept no responsibility for any such changes.

A catalog record for this book is available from the Library of Congress.

ISBN: HB: 979-8-8818-4240-6
ePDF: 979-8-7651-5649-0
eBook: 979-8-7651-5985-9

Typeset by Deanta Global Publishing Services, Chennai, India
Printed and bound in the United States of America

For product safety related questions contact productsafety@bloomsbury.com.

To find out more about our authors and books visit www.bloomsbury.com and sign up for our newsletters.

This book is dedicated to my grandmother, Viv, who shared her joyous wonder with me, to my father who loved hawks, and to my cat buddy, Ivan, who welcomed me to his world of wonders.

CONTENTS

Introduction: Writing the Book I Couldn't Find 1

PART I My Story of Healing Through Wonder 7

    Hope, Wonder, and Comfort: Encounters with Wild Birds 7

1. The Providence of Herons 11
   Disappearing into the Light 11
   Tricks of Light 16
   The Blue Heron 20
   Back to My Senses 24

2. Learning from Herons 29
   Failing Psychotherapy 29
   What Herons Taught Me 35
   My Blue Notebook 43

3. Finding Peace Through Wonder 49
   Building on Strengths 49
   The Luna Moth and the Butterfly 53
   Maine 56

4. Reclaiming My Sense of Wonder 63
   My Little Book of Wonders 63
   Discovering the Neuroscience of Awe and Wonder 69
   Sharing Moments of Wonder with Others 80

PART II Stories of Healing Through Wonder 85

    Introducing Four Wondrous Profiles 85

5 Robyn Houston-Bean: Living with Uncertainty Through Awe and Wonder 89
    Robyn's Story 90
    The Dragonfly 92
    Sharing Awe and Wonder in Relationships and Groups 95
    How Wonder Helps Us Live with Uncertainty 99
    Robyn's Wonder Wisdom in a Nutshell 107

6 Luke Schmaltz: Finding Wonder in Everyday Conversations 111
    Luke's Story 111
    The Wonder of Voice 115
    The Art of Finding Wonder in People 120
    Luke's Wonder Wisdom in a Nutshell 124

7 Carol Bowers: Healing Through Sharing Awe and Wonder 127
    Carol's Story 128
    Jeff 131
    Holding On 134
    The Healing Power of Sharing Awe with Others 138
    Carol's Wonder Wisdom in a Nutshell 141

8 Ricky Allen: The Awe-Inspiring Kindness of a Stranger 145
    Ricky's Story 145
    A Second Chance Put into Action 152
    How Awe Inspires Us to Care for Others 153
    Ricky's Wonder Wisdom in a Nutshell 156

PART III The Healing Power of Awe and Wonder 159

   Opening to Wonder: An Invitation 159

9 Bringing Awe and Wonder into Our Lives 163
   Protecting Our Sense of Wonder in a Cynical World 163
   The Worlds of Wonder Around Us 166

10 Resilience and Community Through Awe and Wonder 191
   A Red-Tailed Hawk 191
   A Willingness to Be Amazed 197
   Paths to Resilience 199
   Creating Community Through Awe and Wonder 206

Appendix: A Friendly Guide to Wondrous Things 211
Acknowledgments 231
Index 234
About the Author 242

Introduction
Writing the Book I Couldn't Find

No matter how busily my mind is chattering away, when I spot a blue heron flying over me, I'm suddenly quiet with wonder. I stop and behold the grace of the bird's wide wings gliding into the wind, and my day begins anew—as a beholder of wonder. My love of herons sparks my sense of awe, openness, and reverence, qualities that I've kept private and sacred in watery sanctuaries where herons thrive.

As a survivor of complex trauma, domestic violence, and many losses, my adoration of herons and wildlife has instilled a sense of meaning, solace, and peace—and given me the will to live. Indeed, my sense of belonging to the natural world has saved my life when I've lost faith in belonging to the human world.

During the lockdown of the Covid-19 pandemic, I rediscovered an unpublished manuscript I'd written twenty-five years ago about my awe-inspiring encounters with herons. Reading my eco-spiritual reflections, I immersed myself in a treasure trove of recollections of my years in Maine and Virginia when I hiked and explored the coastal, marshy habitats of water birds. Wandering and watching herons quietly in their presence, I marveled at their stillness standing in shallow waters, their determination in building nests with their mates, their elegance dancing in pairs during courtship, fishing, preening, and flying. I learned lessons from herons about dignity, balance, grace, patience, the art of timing, and much more—so much so that I was inspired to write a new version of my manuscript about the wondrous experiences that had been vital to my recovery from trauma and loss.

More recently, gazing through my window at maple trees sparkling in a burst of sunshine after a rain shower, I had an epiphany—a moment of awe in its own right. I realized it was my sense of wonder that had kept me strong all these decades, not only those glorious herons. My ability to be amazed by the vastness of the sky, the wilderness, or music, poetry, art, dreams, unexpected acts of kindness, and *many* other wondrous things gave me the will to move forward.

In praise of (and in awe of) our sense of wonder that restores us as survivors of trauma and loss, I've been energized and hopeful while writing this book that is part memoir and part guide. I explore the power of moments that take our breath away and open our minds. In a post-pandemic, cynical world where many of us have lost faith in humanity or lost time doomscrolling through social media, we often forget our sense of wonder or minimize it—but we need to preserve our life-affirming wonder in these uncertain times.

Though previously underexplored and underappreciated, the healing power of wonder has been validated by neuroscience. Now researchers echo what ecologist Rachel Carson believed was essential for human survival: "Those who contemplate the beauty of the earth find reserves of strength that will endure as long as life lasts" (*Silent Spring*, 1962). It's in this spirit that I've written this book, dedicated to the resilience-building gifts of awe and wonder for trauma survivors as well as those living with grief.

Although I've found many books in praise of awe and wonder over the past few years, I've yet to see a book written about the healing power of awe that specifically pertains to survivors of trauma and loss. As a survivor myself, only recently did I realize how much my lifelong capacity for wonder had been so vital to my well-being—indeed, to my very survival. No one I'd known had ever validated my experiences of awe and wonder as a sign of strength, wisdom, or even maturity. When I finally recognized how *essential* my ability to be wowed and amazed had been to my recovery, I was eager to encourage fellow survivors to reclaim their sense of wonder.

Reassured and heartened by the neuroscience research that validates wonder as a source of strength, I now *unabashedly celebrate wonder with others.*

In Part I of this book, I share my own story, weaving in my heron encounters and wildlife experiences, and reclaiming my sense of wonder as my source of resilience. (However, I am careful not to share the actual names of certain friends, family members, or other close relationships, due to privacy and ethical concerns.)

As I developed this book, I ventured out on a storytelling project for trauma and loss survivors by partnering with several organizations in the recovery community. I called this initiative the "Healing Through Wonder Project." Teaming up with Robyn Houston-Bean, founder of the Sun Will Rise Foundation, a peer grief support organization, I was thrilled to have dozens of contributors offering to tell their "wonder stories" of healing encounters. In a matter of months, Robyn and I created a YouTube channel as our storytelling platform, and soon we were sharing a wide variety of awe and wonder experiences through our videos and meetings.

I partnered with several recovery organizations in the Boston area for this storytelling project founded on sincere, heartfelt accounts of moments of awe that changed lives. Part II of this book is a culmination of my storytelling venture with the "Healing Through Wonder Project," in which I present four profiles of storytellers who are survivors of loss, addiction, and trauma.

In Part III, inspired by what I've learned from the people I profiled, by neuroscience research, and by insights on my own journey, I offer guidance for rediscovering wonder in the world and restoring our sense of wonder in ourselves.

Most importantly, as a survivor of trauma and loss, and as other survivors in my book inspire us, I encourage the generous act of sharing our wonder experiences with *each other*, such as storytelling about a moment of awe, or taking a walk together, vibing together to music at a concert, watching a sunset, or reading poetry out loud—a whole new level of healing is sparked by shared awe and wonder.

Writing this book has given me the opportunity to better understand how awe and wonder heal us by interweaving the neuroscience of wonder with breathtaking experiences of awe from survivors of trauma and loss. Tying the research to our stories, I could clearly identify and validate the ways that awe and wonder had carried us through our long struggle through recovery. It was heartening to claim that even one awe-inspiring moment that took our breath away could spark our sense of purpose and belonging in the world.

It might be useful to point out that this book focuses primarily on the positive, optimal qualities of awe in terms of how neuroscience describes well-being and prosocial behaviors. I discuss the actionable and meaningful aspects of awe and wonder as pathways to resilience.

This book does not explore the wide world of psychedelics as a source of awe. This topic is a separate domain that is outside of my purview considering my expertise as a rehabilitation counselor, educator, and support group facilitator. In the book's collection of firsthand accounts and stories of healing, I emphasize the natural thrill, joy, and connection of sharing wonder-infused moments.

Stories of wonder, awe, enchantment, and reverence that had been secretly tucked away for decades are generously offered to readers of this book. I conclude by proclaiming that our well-being thrives on our willingness to open ourselves to encounters of awe and wonder, no matter how brief or fleeting or odd—in the sky, on a beach, in a candlelit ceremony, in a song. There's a whole, wide, dazzling world to amaze us beyond the thicket of our overthinking minds, algorithms, and cluttered screens. As Mary Oliver beckons us in her poem, "Wild Geese," we can look up and follow the calls of the geese, "harsh and exciting—over and over announcing our place in the family of things."

And as for the herons I adore, and as a survivor of trauma, I can attest to the faith of Terry Tempest Williams: "I pray to the birds because they remind me of what I love rather than what I fear. And at the end of my prayers, they teach me how to listen" (*Refuge: An Unnatural History of Family and Place*).

PART I

MY STORY OF HEALING THROUGH WONDER

Hope, Wonder, and Comfort: Encounters with Wild Birds

For many thousands of years in all cultures, wild birds have beckoned our sense of wonder in fascinating ways: as signs of hope, spirits of deceased loved ones, totems, angels, muses, or as exquisite creatures to adore. Our encounters with birds have often offered a fresh, clean chance for awe and wonder to restore our lives.

Not only have I loved blue herons for decades, I've also been inspired by accounts of human encounters with herons across many cultures and centuries. Famously, the Egyptians worshiped the Bennu, a type of heron embodying creation and rebirth that flew across the Nile into the rising sun, entering the realms of the afterlife, and returning to earth at sunset.

St. Columba of Scotland, around AD 560, found an injured heron after a storm and carried it back to his monastery, where his fellow monks cared for its injuries. They learned a message of divine faith after the heron was strong enough to fly off to Ireland and return every spring to their monastery.

Native Americans prayed to herons before their hunts as they revered the bird's patience, good judgment, and brilliant sense of timing. The Hitchiti Tribe of the Muscogee-speaking people of Georgia teach the lesson of the patient, determined, and wise heron in their *Heron and Hummingbird* tale.

Heron lore includes classic, beloved short stories, such as *A White Heron* by Sarah Orne Jewett, and poems by Mary Oliver, Longfellow, Elizabeth Bishop, and more.

Long before the internet and before the popularity and mass consumption of finding our totem birds and spirit animals, I was drawn to herons. My calling to follow herons is a pure and soulful yearning that comes from a sense of reverence for the mysteries of life.

Most of us love birds and cherish a particular bird that sparks our sense of awe. My grandmother Viv adored chickadees, and my mother perked up every time she saw a purple martin near her kitchen window. My father revered red-tailed hawks, and my sister could sit on her balcony and watch blue jays for hours.

When I see a chickadee, I remember my grandmother. Through every single characteristic of that chatty bird, through its movements and songs, the trees it favors—through these delicate, tiny details, I hold the everlasting essence of my grandmother, who left this world forty-five years ago.

Stopping to notice a favorite bird of a loved one gives us ways to see our person in a whole new light. And these fleeting moments of discovery restore ourselves.

1

The Providence of Herons

Were the birds better friends than their hunter might have been,—who can tell?
Whatever treasures were lost to her, woodlands and summertime, remember!
—SARAH ORNE JEWETT, *A WHITE HERON AND OTHER STORIES*

Disappearing into the Light

As a wildly idealistic and empathic child in the 1960s, my openhearted acts of kindness lacked discretion and good judgment. My starry-eyed zeal to save the world and help the wretched led to altruistic misadventures that left me unpopular and alone.

In the woods near my house, I played my song flute and danced in praise of splendid entities with wings: angels, fairies, spirits, sprites, chickadees, white butterflies, swans, or gods such as Zephyrus and Hermes. At my ballet recitals, where my grandmother and mother sat smiling, I twirled in winged ecstasy, flitting in toe shoes and swirling in shimmering chiffon.

Pale, thin, flighty, fidgety, with intense blue eyes and wispy blonde hair, I looked as if I'd just landed on Earth from some rare, celestial accident. Ungrounded, disassociated from my body—scarcely touching the earth, I hardly wanted to be in this world. Most people found my nerdy spirituality strange, perplexing, if not obnoxious. My wondrous, wide-eyed propensity for being wowed and my eagerness to share my amazement never seemed to fit normal daily conversations.

Fortunately, my grandmother Viv enjoyed my wondrous musings and spiritual proselytizing as we snapped string beans or folded laundry on her screened porch. She listened patiently and only stopped me when she heard busy, chattering chickadees, her favorite birds. "There they go again, talking up a storm, just like you." She shrugged, chuckled, shook her head in wonderment, and I stopped talking. We listened to the chickadees for a moment. I loved her awe-inspired expressions as we allowed the chickadees and the cacophony of other singing birds to join in their evening chorus.

After a minute, she turned and looked intently at me. "Now, where in the world do you get all these spiritual ideas? They sure don't come from your mother or father!"

No one ever knew the source of my spiritual hunger for the miraculous and the mystical. I'd never trusted anyone enough to tell of my early encounter with heaven until I told Viv when I was seventeen. In Potomac, Maryland, sitting close to her on her patio surrounded by marigolds and asters on a balmy August evening, I confided my long-held secret of a near-death experience.

At the age of five, I almost drowned in a swimming pool. I remember my lungs about to burst, then suddenly finding myself comforted by a cocoon-like rapture into which I collapsed. Scientists may describe my near-death experience as an explosion of endorphins, but I attribute this phenomenon while dying to biochemistry as well as to God. Why not both? Whatever happened to me as I disappeared into immense light felt as natural and sacred as falling in love. We fall deeply in love with whatever saves us from excruciating pain.

Not yet having learned to swim, I floated in an inner tube in a neighbor's small swimming pool, though I could hear my mother and father yelling in an argument from the back porch. I drifted and wiggled in my inner tube until I accidentally slipped right through it and quickly sank down to the bottom of the pool. My feet touched the rough surface of the pool, and I tried to jump high enough to reach the surface of the water. Several feet above me, I could plainly see the surface of the water, yet it was too far to push myself upward to get to the vital air above it. With all my might and energy, I tried to get my head above water, but I just couldn't make it. My legs dissolved into muscle spasms until I was unable to move, and I sank again.

Lying on the bone-hard surface at the bottom of the pool, feeling cold and heavy, I fixed my eyes above me where air met water. This edge between water and air began to glisten and glow prism-like, entrancing me. Yet my lungs tortured me. I screamed through my eyes for someone to save me. Any moment now, my father might dive down to me. But no one came to the surface of the water. I waited. I kept watching. Through the water, I could only see a ball of sun in a wide pale blue sky.

The sun grew into a glimmering white light, reaching through the surface of the water, sending its rays towards me and wrapping me in a gleaming, warm blanket. By its sheer beauty and luster, I lost my fear and allowed the blanket of light to hold me as if in the arms of a giant loving angel. My forehead felt kissed by its presence, and my heart filled with pure love in this embrace. So peaceful and comforted, I closed my eyes and let myself be rocked softly in the waves of light and water around me. I heard a resonant voice clearly guiding me, "Close your eyes and let me take you to the sun." This angelic force of light lifted me above my small, drowning body and carried me into the sky until we were flying towards the sun. I became one with the sun and felt myself pulled into the heavens. Without my body, I seemed to be disappearing, yet I grew immensely alive and radiant as I merged into a wider and greater ocean of light.

Suddenly, I was pulled away from the light by my father's strong arms as I gasped for air, coughed, and clung to his warm, wet shoulders. How starkly different his tense body felt compared to the soft light of the other world I had briefly visited. My father carried me for a little while, trembling, rocking me a bit, as I looked up to the sun. Though my father had rescued me from drowning and brought me back into this world, I hesitated to completely reenter this existence. Betwixt and between two worlds, I only halfheartedly entered my human body on this earth—and lived in this liminal space for another ten years.

Indeed, I was spacey, and people didn't like that. People didn't seem to like me at all in the hostile and chaotic household where I had to survive. Anyone could attack me, unexpectedly, physically, verbally, and I never quite knew when it was coming, despite my hypervigilance. Pale, skinny, and scared of human interaction, better to hide and stay out of trouble. I dared not look anyone directly in the eyes or say anything wrong. I kept my head down and made myself small with hunched shoulders to avoid contact so effectively that, by the age of twelve, I was actually smaller than my younger siblings and appeared physically underdeveloped. It was dangerous to inhabit my little body, let alone grow in it.

It was safest just to disappear.

After my near-death experience, in my betwixt-and-between existence, I could easily dissociate from my body and the people in my household. I could run away to the woods near our house to protect myself and hear myself think. I built forts in the woods far from people, far from harm, to immerse myself in picture books about Greek gods or write poems and draw in little notebooks.

The only human being I trusted was my grandmother, Viv, who gently hugged me and rubbed my back to soothe my frequent stomach aches; otherwise, I lived in my otherworldliness. From age four to twenty-four, I clung to a disembodied form of spirituality, a defense mechanism of spiritual bypassing that served as an imaginary escape from the harshness of my daily reality.

I twice rescued poor, writhing mice from cats that bit me and gave me rabies (for which I had tetanus shots). In front of classmates, amid giggles and sneers, I recited my poems of flying with angels or gave speeches to save the starving babies of Biafra. I tried a few times to offer comforting words to bullied classmates, but they winced and ran away. I made sure any ladybug crawling beside my bed was carefully handled and released outside my window (until my annoyed sister threatened to smash the bugs herself). I identified with Saint

Francis of Assisi, Jesus, and self-sacrificing heroes such as Gandhi, Mother Teresa, and Joan of Arc, who lived for their missions instead of themselves.

My dissociative, disembodied spirituality was a survival reaction to complex trauma as well as the loneliness of enduring that trauma alone. Thankfully, my loving human bond with Viv allowed a sense of safety to come back into my body. Otherwise, with a spiritual rationale for denial, I could rise above the fray—just as my near-death experience had so brilliantly proved to me. I became quite adept at spiritual bypassing over cruelty, fears, and dangers. I believed I could protect myself with white light, a belief that gave me a false sense of protection and led me to more danger. Whether it was my overactive imagination or my ability to immerse myself in out-of-body experiences, as a starry-eyed seeker, I fell in love with the rampant New Age spirituality of the 1970s.

Tricks of Light

In 1978, at twenty-three years old, in a New Age bookstore in Richmond, Virginia, I met a lanky, long-haired, bearded man, about forty years old, sitting near the checkout counter. He asked if I'd like my astrological chart done.

"How much?" I asked.

"Twenty dollars. I'll give you a sample for ten minutes." He was ready for business.

"Okay, sure."

He directed me. "Please tell me your birthday, where you were born, and at what time."

"October 18, 1954, in Lexington, Virginia, at 2:30 p.m.—I think."

Before I knew it, I was sitting in a dim, tiny room at the back of the bookstore. He opened a huge tome called an ephemeris across a table. He drew the signs and planets of my natal chart on tracing paper with colored pencils. Suddenly, he looked up at me and shook his head in amazement.

"Wow. Your sun is conjunct Neptune in Libra. You're probably psychic. What do you think of that?"

I was enthralled. "Well, could be true... are *you* psychic?"

He smiled and echoed me. "Well, could be true."

This conversation was the start of many meetings with him at the diner near the bookstore. His name was Dan, and he was a popular local astrologer who followed the teachings of the guru Satchidananda and was a friend of someone in the Rainbow Family in Oregon. Impressed with Dan's associations, metaphysical knowledge, and professed IQ of 155, I ventured to tell him about my childhood near-death experience and other supernatural encounters I'd had in the woods—stories that even Viv didn't know about. I'd read Raymond Moody's bestselling hit *Life After Life* about near-death experiences, and I was bursting to tell Dan all the ways this book rang true for me. He listened closely, and I spoke freely. He was a friend, a kindred spirit. I'd known Dan in a past life.

I'd never been in love with anyone before. But soon, within weeks, as he read my life's destiny through tarot cards and numerology, I fell for his mesmerizing, electric gray eyes, and gentle little hugs. In his candlelit studio, after reading out loud passages from *A Course in Miracles*, and after slowly rubbing Aura Glow oil on my feet and between my toes, I lost my virginity to him.

A few months later, I followed him out to Eugene, Oregon, after he had joined the Rainbow Gatherings, a counterculture series of festivals and events connected to the Rainbow Family community. He was able to make a small fortune as an astrologer and tarot reader at their many spiritual events, but he also started a relationship with another woman, whom he dazzled with his metaphysical prowess. Soon after securing a housecleaning job and barely scraping by, and realizing I was pregnant, I confronted him about his other lover from the Rainbow Family and begged him for money for an abortion. He suddenly turned violent, almost choking me to death.

Days later, I flew back to Virginia to escape him, underwent an abortion, and quickly found a new job working as an activity aide at a hospital.

But he returned to Virginia and stalked me for weeks, following me to where I worked, knowing my tracks from my apartment, and figuring out how to break in through a basement window. He threatened me with a knife and held me captive for a month. I had to quit my job, disconnect my phone, and give him sex. Finally, escaping while he slept one morning at 3:00 a.m., I ended up broke, homeless, and without a car.

I was too afraid of him to risk my life speaking up to the police. He would only get worse if he found out. My grandmother Viv was worried about me, but she was strapped taking care of my grandfather, who had just had a stroke. I dared not go near her home or else Dan, knowing where she lived, might come after us. Domestic violence shelters for women did not exist in Richmond, Virginia, until later in

1979—too late for me. Women like me were left to their own devices to find shelter and safety.

I dashed off to Florida on an Amtrak train with cash from my sister to stay with my father. Shockingly, the very next night after I arrived, he told me the news that Viv had just died of a heart attack. She had been driving my grandfather to a doctor's appointment and had to pull off the road. Raw in his grief and rage, my father bitterly stated that she shouldn't have been worried about my "predicament" with my abusive boyfriend on top of the stress of taking care of my grandfather. He added, "She's always been worried about you."

In tears, I withdrew from him and ran outside to sit alone in the dark where no one could find me. I was up all night, wishing I were dead, in the throes of grief twisted with guilt over the death of my grandmother. Meanwhile, Dan was still in my apartment that he had taken over, just waiting for another opportunity to attack and control me.

A few days later, pale, thin, tense with stomach cramps, I returned to Virginia with my father after a miserable, long car ride to Viv's funeral. All seemed a blur around me as I stared blankly across the candles throughout the ceremony. Afterwards, fortunately, I could stay a few more days to rest with an aunt. During that time, my mother and one of her friends took action to contact the Richmond police to have Dan arrested and taken from my apartment. He was given a restraining order, and I was offered various sofas and futons to crash on by sympathetic cousins and neighbors.

By this point, exhausted, traumatized by Dan, and grief-stricken over Viv, I could barely support myself by cleaning houses as I struggled to get back on my feet.

But suicidal thoughts plagued me while I scrubbed and mopped kitchens and bathrooms alone in empty houses for hours on end. I could shine up a soap dish or polish a silver tray, but I couldn't escape the self-loathing, shame, and guilt for being such a loser—such a sucker. I'd fallen for Dan's charms and abuse along with all the dazzling New Age spirituality and Rainbow Gathering nonsense. I'd fallen in love with light and angels, enchanted by my own near-death experience, but none of that glorious light could ever protect me on earth. At the root of it all, breaking my heart, I'd gravely disappointed and worried the one person I trusted and adored, Viv.

She had died, worried sick about me and my miserable life.

The Blue Heron

I had a plan to end my life, and I knew of a secluded place to carry out my plan.

With no car and a little cash, I hitchhiked to a desolate former campground on the James River, many miles east of Richmond. I carried in my bag a bottle of cheap red wine, a plastic cup, and a bottle of Valium, all stolen from my mother.

Like some kind of bum, I sat on a tree stump and poured the sweet red wine into my cup. I made sure no one was around. I found a soft patch of grass on the bank of the river.

In the twilight, I nestled into the cool grass. I swallowed a couple of pills. (I could take all the pills after I finished the wine.) But love and grief for my grandmother filled my heart so deeply that I curled up on the ground and sobbed. I wanted to disappear into the softness of the soil beneath the grass and moss. Lying on my stomach, breathing in the moist air from the river, I felt my heart beating, pulsing into the heart of the earth. I allowed the earth to hold me as a breeze blanketed me across the backs of my legs, my back, the top of my shoulders, and the top of my head. I wanted to release all my pain and let it flow out of me to any place where the earth could absorb it.

When the silver light of a thin crescent moon rose over the river, I turned to my side and gazed at the shimmering reflection.

I lost my sense of time and my tears stopped falling. Lying in a delicate stillness, I listened to the mourning doves sing their twilight song. The breeze grew stronger and cooler as a large bird flew towards me and circled above me. I looked up, sat up, and I could just make out that it was a great blue heron. She hovered over me, almost pausing, watching me, intent on landing close by. I sensed she was a female heron headed to her nest in the pines of the neighboring marsh. Yet instead of keeping course towards the marsh, she suddenly angled out of her flight and turned towards me, landing only about ten feet away. Amazing, I thought how enormous and tall she was—and so close! I could see in detail her gray-blue feathers, now dappled with silvery dew. Her slightly coiled neck revealed a fine line of tiny white feathers in her profile. Her yellow eyes on me, fierce and keen, humbled me in receiving her full gaze. I dared to look right into her eyes and felt a wave of human self-consciousness. We became entranced, eye-to-eye, soul-to-soul, holding each other in rapt attention.

Time stopped. She drew me in more as she lifted her head high, uncoiling her neck. I instinctively lifted my head. She majestically spread her wings, still keeping her eyes on me. As if calling me to fly with her, I watched and waited for her next move. She took a few slow steps closer toward me. She tilted her head slightly as if with curiosity.

The heron took another elegant step. Long breezes rising off the river enveloped us, blowing my hair and blowing her feathers at once. Even when I blinked, the heron seemed to blink, and the longer I kept still, the longer the heron stayed with me. The heron took another step closer, appearing to trust me.

Awestruck, everything inside my mind stopped. The clamor of voices in my head and the human drama I had been acting out suddenly ended, as if I were waking up from an anguished dream. The heron took another step towards me, and I sensed she felt my reverence for her. I slightly bowed my head in deep gratitude and wonderment. She spread her wings, then opened and closed them a few times until she pushed off the ground and leaped into the sky. She flew low over the wide river at first, then slowly rose higher as she headed toward the western horizon.

I sat still, stunned, and glowing. I could hardly fathom what had just happened—why had this wild bird come so close to me? Why, at this time, at this particular moment, when I was ready to swallow the remaining pills in the bottle? Perhaps I didn't appear threatening, or perhaps it was because I stayed so patient and still. Perhaps it was because I had given up my own life and was open to anything to take me out of the grip of my tormenting thoughts.

Or was she the spirit of my grandmother? Or an angel or a sign sent from her?

But the beauty of the flowing river, the deep, twilight blue of this sky, and the crescent moon crowning me was enough of an answer. Indeed, it was a blessing. It didn't matter if I ever knew why this bird had come so close to me. What a wonderful mystery! Beholding her shining majesty in the moonlight had taken my breath away, waking me out of the trance of my death wish.

I gently stood up and walked slowly along the river, feeling fortunate that I'd been energized by the magic of this moment, no matter how fleeting my encounter with the heron had been. How could I ever believe I was alone in this world with so much life around me! How could I believe God or divinity was just an idea in someone's religion or a channeled spirit in a New Age book when a heron had come so close to me? No matter how tragic my life had been, she had called me to join her wider world of breezy skies, splashing rivers, waving grasses, and shining pines. How dare I squander this radiance on earth!

I *did* want to live, after all. I could live in this world that the heron had beckoned me to rediscover. Until now, I had believed I was a defective, failed person. But standing under the stars at this moment, I was in my own element, in my glory, and grateful for my life!

I dumped all the remaining pills in the bottle of Valium into the river. I watched them float away, bubbling in the rippling water. I made a vow to Viv, holding my hands up to the sky, declaring out loud that I wanted to live.

And I told her that I wouldn't try to end my life ever again. I promised I would return to the watery sanctuaries of herons if I ever felt the pull of my death wish. I had the power to walk to the water's edge of a river or stream, pond, or ocean, in any town or city where I lived. I would make pilgrimages to their providence to reclaim my right to belong in this world.

I was ready to leave the campground and walk back for four miles to the bus station to travel back to Richmond.

Back to My Senses

On my days off from cleaning houses, I wandered to places where herons thrived. At James River Park, near Belle Isle, herons fished in glimmering waters while I perched myself on long flat rocks jutting off the island amid the swirling falls of the river. I lost myself in lavender and golden skies that reflected in shallow pools of water over smooth, rounded stones. I learned the evening rhythms, calls, and routines of many other birds as I wrote down my thoughts in a small notebook carried in my pocket.

The behaviors I observed in herons and other birds taught me lessons about the art of timing and inspired me to write my reflections on the saving grace of divine timing.

I marveled at the patience, stillness, and amazing sense of timing the herons exhibited as they fished. They always knew the perfect moment when the fish arrived. With graceful positioning, waiting, aiming, wading, waiting again, then darting to their prey, they knew exactly when to act and when not to act. They could spot an opportunity and wait for the right moment without chasing it. It fascinated me how their brilliant, delicate sense of timing and stunningly accurate aim with their long beaks were vital to their survival.

Indeed, this patient sense of timing and mindful focus learned from the herons was key to my grounding and recovery from grief and trauma.

I reflected on the art of timing, an underappreciated skill in our hectic culture that pushed us to get what we wanted when we wanted it and have it our way (as the TV ads said). But as every skillful archer or fisherman knows, the faster we chase after our prey, the more we lose our sense of timing, grounding, and focus, and miss our opportunities. Timing requires respect for the wisdom, rhythms, and cycles of nature. And this sense of timing is essential to healing from pain.

With the patience and stillness I learned from the herons, I reassured myself that I could take the time I needed to heal from my grief and soothe my agitated, jangly body by simply slowing down. Slowing down, breathing fully, walking with solid footing, and moving mindfully were essential steps to my grounding and relief from the tension that I didn't need to carry. When I sat with the herons in their watery sanctuaries, I embraced all the time I needed and gave myself the gift of time. I didn't need to force myself to change or force myself to move too fast for anyone, even for myself—because force had always backfired for me. This deep, gentle sense of patience, timing, and acceptance allowed me to fully be in my body and take up space on this earth. I had the right to solidly inhabit my body. I could hold my head high like the herons, stand still, and stand tall against the currents of life's flow.

Back at my housecleaning jobs, I noticed my balance, focus, and coordination had improved, as I was practicing what I had learned from the herons. I realized I truly enjoyed cleaning and tidying up people's homes because I could immediately see the results—and so did my clients! With new referrals for other clients who were art professors at Virginia Commonwealth University, I thoroughly immersed myself in cleaning their art studios, as well as watering their plants or feeding their cats when they were out of town.

I often thought of Viv and imagined she would be pleased to see me feeling better, finding satisfaction in my work, and saving money to return to college for a Bachelor of Fine Arts degree in dance and theater. I yearned to teach dance and drama to children.

One day, at the home of one of the art professors, as I dusted their many watercolors of birds framed exquisitely in their den, I discovered a portrait of a chickadee on a fence. I thought of how Viv loved chickadees, and I shed a few tears. And yet, after wiping my eyes, I marveled at the delicacy and love the artist had put forth to create this lovely painting. The browns and yellows and blacks had been so precisely swept across the paper that I could almost see the breeze across the feathers of this tiny bird.

I paused and realized that I would like to meet the person who painted this chickadee. Was it the owner of this house I was cleaning, or was it a friend or a relative? I decided to stay a few minutes longer than usual after the house was completely cleaned. It was now 5:00 on an October evening. I sat down at the kitchen table by the window, basking in the glowing autumn light. I decided to wait a bit to see if perhaps I could meet whoever came home soon.

My timing was right. The wife of the professor who owned this house, Jill, greeted me and immediately remarked on the good smell of the Murphy Oil Soap I had just used to wash her cabinets.

"Oh my, that smells good!"

"I love it, too," I chimed in.

She smiled. "It's nice to actually meet you for a change! You're usually gone by this time."

"Well, to be honest, I waited to ask you something, and I hope you don't mind . . . but I was curious to know who painted those lovely watercolors of birds in your den?"

"*I* did." She beamed. "I never went to art school, and my degree is in social work, but I love birds and watercolors, so I just do this as a labor of love."

"I really adore your chickadee," I humbly added.

"Me too." She chuckled, then paused with a wistful expression. "My grandmother loved chickadees. I always think of her when I hear their calls outside."

"My grandmother loved chickadees too."

"Really?" She was intrigued.

"*Really!*" I could hardly speak.

Jill invited me to stay a while longer to chat and offered me a cup of Red Zinger tea. She held up her teapot and added, "I'd like to put a little cider in it too."

I accepted her offer. We talked tenderly about our grandmothers for over an hour as the rays of the setting sun poured across the kitchen table, spreading across our faces and across the shiny wooden cabinets I'd just cleaned. We marveled at the ways our grandmothers had shared our unabashed, joyous, and wondrous encounters with birds.

Reminiscing with Jill was the beginning of a long friendship that has lasted to this day.

2

Learning from Herons

Everything that is in the heavens, on earth, and under the earth is penetrated with connectedness, penetrated with relatedness.
—HILDEGARD OF BINGEN

Failing Psychotherapy

A year after Dan had been arrested, I kept my life simple, quiet, mostly alone, managing to create little rituals of self-care alongside my five housecleaning gigs. The structure and control I needed in my life depended on maintaining steady and reliable services for my clients as well as their pets, plants, and neighbors. I continued to avoid socializing, dating, or venturing into new activities. My solitary days gently afforded warm stretches of tranquil walks and writing in my journal. That was all I wanted—and all I could handle.

But I still suffered frequent nightmares in which Dan appeared to taunt and terrorize me. In these marathon dreams, he captured me with demonic eyes and telepathic remote control, forcing me to do whatever he wanted as his own plaything. Other abusive people from my childhood stood by his side, mocking me, teasing, poking—until I awoke, sweating feverishly, and feeling completely drained.

In the dark early hours of those mornings after the night terrors, nagging thoughts returned, voicing their commands to end my life. I could briefly suppress these inner demons by sipping two strong cups of French roast coffee and flipping through the pages of a *Mademoiselle* or *Cosmopolitan* magazine. Next, I would put on my flannel shirt, jeans, and sneakers, grab an apple, and dash off on my bicycle to clean my clients' houses.

I didn't realize at the time that I was undergoing PTSD and major depression. Viv had died over a year earlier, and without her, I had no one to confide in about the state of my mental health. I ruminated on the victim-blaming words of my raging father. I bitterly replayed in my thoughts the ways I had been left to my own devices to save myself from Dan until my family had seen me at Viv's funeral. In their eyes, I'd often attracted the "wrong types," so I'd made my own bed to lie in. I must have been too soft and weak.

I festered in the tormenting truth that human beings could be incredibly cruel and indifferent, and that our communities did little to protect victims of violence. My rug of humanity had been pulled out from under me, not only once but throughout my life. On shaky ground, easily rattled, I lived with rampant insecurity inside of me and a lack of protection outside of me.

In social interactions, I tried to compensate for my anxious, darting eyes with forced cheerfulness that usually backfired into nervous laughter, awkward remarks, and apologies. Some people called the look on my face "scared bunny eyes." With such high-pitched guardedness, I lost my concentration when people explained things to me, quickly forgot their names, or spaced out on their instructions and directions. Sometimes I blanked out so badly that I suddenly excused myself with a disappearing act such as running to the bathroom, stepping outside, or just leaving entirely.

What people didn't understand about traumatic stress is that it stuck around like shreds of shrapnel in our neuromuscular system, our reflexes, and biochemistry. Little was known at that time about the neurological damage of trauma. No matter how hard I tried to stay calm, that scared bunny look would come over my face and ruin my chances of appearing confident or stable.

It came down to this: *People scared me most of the time.*

Desperate to alleviate my fear of people and the hypervigilance that exhausted me, I tried several months of psychotherapy with two clinicians. At first, they seemed to warmly welcome my attempts to describe my ordeal with Dan. But instead of validating my terror and grief, these therapists, though smiling and friendly, questioned and scrutinized my "poor choices." I had to explain why I'd fallen in love with a monster like Dan and how I'd been duped by New Age spiritual teachings. I had to justify why I panicked when I stepped onto the street on my way home in the darkening sky, or when a gas station attendant smirked at me, or when a housekeeping client complained about the way I folded their linens.

The questioning ("why" questions) by these therapists made me feel foolish and inadequate, and worse, their scrutiny exposed how utterly alone I was in defending my choices. When I tried to explain what I was doing to recover from the trauma of domestic violence, my coping methods were discounted as avoidance and escapism. In one therapy session, I shared a passage from my journal about a serenely beautiful river walk alone, and the therapist responded, "That's lovely, but you're avoiding people by escaping to nature." According to her, my sense of wonder and reverence for nature could not be validated as a source of strength because these were not interpersonal experiences. I was told I should learn assertiveness and boundary-setting skills—and not simply avoid relationships by "withdrawing to the woods." Her dismissal of the solace and grounding I felt from my awe-inspiring times in nature did indeed shut me down from sharing anything authentic or intimate about myself. I didn't dare risk telling her how a blue heron had saved me from overdosing on Valium, or how my sanctuary by the river restored my will to live.

Should I have told this therapist that the person who *did* appreciate my sense of wonder and love of the natural world was my grandmother, Viv? We shared moments of awe every day and embraced our wonderment—*together*. How I missed her! But now, after her death, in front of a therapist, I could hardly mention her without sobbing—too much for me to handle. Dare I show these therapists how fragile I was or how ashamed I was for being this fragile? Could they at least appreciate that I was still standing and still willing to talk to them at all?

Sadly, I blamed myself for failing at psychotherapy, although, decades later, I've realized that psychotherapy failed me with victim-blaming and pathologizing.

In 1979 and 1980, few therapists had specialized training in domestic violence, let alone PTSD. Assertiveness training and other cognitive/behavioral therapies were beginning to become popular, especially for couples and marital therapy, but trauma was widely misunderstood. Victims of abuse might be coaxed by their therapists in front of their perpetrator/partner to say "no" or set boundaries with assertiveness training in the therapy room, but too often, later at home, the victim ended up in more danger.

Certainly, the vast neuroscience of trauma had not yet emerged until the technology of MRIs (magnetic resonance imaging) navigated the intricate domains of our brains. Judith Herman's groundbreaking book on complex trauma, *Trauma and Recovery*, was published in 1992, and Bessel van der Kolk's widely popular book, *The Body Keeps the Score* was released in 2014, offering an accessible explanation of the impact of trauma on the body. Thankfully, today, research on the brain damage caused by trauma has revolutionized our understanding, resulting in trauma-informed care and extensive awareness of the effects of adverse childhood experiences (ACEs).

But in 1980, long before these breakthroughs in healing trauma and abuse, most therapists tended to look at relational problems (including domestic abuse) as an opportunity to fix poor coping skills or to correct faulty patterns learned in childhood. I was told that I had "ingrained habits" that had caused me to be victimized by Dan. In the eyes of the therapists, the trauma in my childhood had created a self-destructive streak in me that had *attracted* Dan's abuse. I must have had a self-defeating drive in me that gave me "radar for abusers," according to one therapist.

Indeed, I agreed with the clinicians that I should own my own susceptibilities to attracting abusers as defects learned in early childhood. But my ownership of so much damage and the spotlight on these defects was not a solution that gave me confidence, let alone faith, in my (already shattered) self. My true strengths that made me resilient, such as introspection, sensitivity, a sense of wonder, and immense imagination, were not recognized as valid because these were not robust interpersonal attributes. Sure, I could admit to the therapists that my track record with human relationships had been truly shitty so far, aside from my grandmother, who was the one person I'd ever trusted. In short, in the therapist's eyes, my defects far outweighed my strengths.

And worse, my strengths were seen as vulnerabilities that others could exploit. My empathy, my spiritual-seeking qualities, and even my sense of wonder were liabilities. Clinicians discounted my grief and dismay about the New Age spirituality that had misguided me. As I shared with them the teachings of *A Course in Miracles* or other ego-denying, dissociative spiritual practices, they explained with exasperation, "But you must take responsibility for your choices—you *chose* that path."

Often a target of narcissists and sociopaths, young, highly empathic women (empaths) like me were taught to feel ashamed of our softness, compassion, generosity, and idealism that got us into trouble. As victims of violence, we hated ourselves for being so impressionable and gullible when we fell in love, not only with our partners but with God, scripture, angels, gurus, or psychics. In 1980, it was up to the woman *alone* to walk away from the perpetrator, the marriage, the job, the school, the church, or the cult where she was harassed—and to "cut the victim crap," as one therapist insisted.

Those harsh words echoed in my mind every day alongside the inner voice of my father and others who judged me: *Cut the victim crap.* Repeating that command was how I tried to silence the nagging thoughts that shamed my victimhood—which only gave power to that inner demon seething at me for being the victim, perpetuating a vicious cycle.

In those days, suffering as a victim of violence, bullying, mind control, or abuse was not typically viewed systemically, culturally, or as something beyond the agency of the exhausted individual. Grieving or ranting was not tolerated for long by clinicians because healing meant getting over it and moving ahead with a new toolkit of assertiveness skills. Furthermore, I was warned that if I continued to feel weak, hurt, and vulnerable, then I would certainly "attract" another abusive person into my life. So I had to cut that victim crap, get a grip on my weakness, and get strong, or I was doomed to more abuse.

But I *was*, indeed, a victim of abuse, and acutely suffering from trauma. I stopped going to the therapy sessions that focused on my defects, triggering tremendous doubts about my own character as well as my own sanity. If I followed their logic, all the misery of my ordeal with Dan had been *my fault*.

How could a victim of violence heal or grieve if she had so many defects to fix in herself?

What Herons Taught Me

When I followed the herons to their sanctuaries on the James River, the troubling thoughts of my failed psychotherapy, victim-blaming, and shame turned into tears, breaking through a torrent of memories and doubts. When a heron or an osprey flew near me, I felt permission to cry, to tenderly allow little waves of pain to leave my body. On the private tiny beaches by the river, I could whisper as well as softly sob to the oak trees as they trembled in the wind. I grieved the truth that

I'd been a victim of abuse and had been judged when I'd reached out for help.

But after many long, good bouts of crying, a sense of acceptance and self-compassion gently, yet briefly, softened my heart. At least I could claim that I had not given up my will to live. I was still here—in a pocket of sunlight by the swirling currents of the river. I didn't have to justify my existence by claiming to be a decent or strong human being. I belonged with the herons in their lush marshes filled with hundreds of other chattering birds. I could stop watching for something else to go wrong. Here everything shone in the glow of the wide river, even the broken twigs, the fallen hollowed pines, the skin of a snake, or a dead muskrat.

The Necessity of Sanctuaries

The James River Park System provided 380 acres (now 600 acres) of protected habitat for blue herons, eagles, ospreys, owls, ducks, and many more birds. In conservation areas for the herons, clusters of islands in the river were densely packed with trees filled with dozens of nests, surrounded by the rapids and waterfalls of the river.

It struck me that I needed protection and conservation lands as much as these wild birds. Before my healing from trauma could begin, a private, safe place on earth was essential, far from the scrutiny and judgment of people. Instead of trying to change myself, I could first accept myself as I was, away from the opinions and expectations of others. Here it didn't matter if I was thinking bad or good things. I just wanted to watch the herons tending to their own lives. How comforting it was to watch these birds so patiently build their nests, flying to the highest branches, precisely placing each twig upon twig to construct a home for their family!

Gazing upon herons building their heronries across the treetops, I heard the greater hum of birds and insects creating their intricate networks between earth, water, and sky. I felt the serene, comforting presence of a vast life force inside me and all around me at once. This quiet radiance instilled moments of peace, oneness, gratitude, and awe. People may have called this Divine Providence, or grace, the Holy Spirit, Nirvana, Heaven, or bliss. I was blessed that the herons had shown me their providence where I, as a human, could join their greater, wider world that had a place for me.

Clearly, being by water was essential to my spiritual growth. Other people might have preferred mountaintops, deserts, oceans, or a garden. I remember how Jesus loved his olive trees in the garden of Gethsemane, and perhaps he had briefly retreated to Gethsemane when he knew his time on earth was up. Maybe he just wanted to visit those wise ancient trees to speak with God that night before his capture.

Herons took me to my own kind of Gethsemane, my place on earth where I felt the presence of divinity. In such a place, my soul felt free enough to come forth and speak out, guiding me to what was best for my own healing.

Patience and the Art of Timing

On every evening walk, I continued my practice of revering the art of timing and divine timing that I'd learned a year earlier from the herons. As they stood quietly and elegantly fishing in the shallow, rushing waters of the wide river, I stopped to allow the solace of their stillness to sink deep into my body. My previously racing thoughts no longer needed to push for my attention. My mind settled down as my thoughts moved along like little bubbles in the current of the river. Whenever I spent time by the river, I claimed the time I needed for grounding, pacing, and balance.

Balance Between Solitude and Relationships

Another beautiful lesson the herons taught me, as I studied them for hours, was their remarkable versatility of being solitary for long stretches of time yet also being communal. Their lives were balanced between solitude and relationships. In crowded and busy colonies for breeding, nesting, and parenting, they lived in social seasons in great contrast to the months they spent alone.

In their family and communal times, herons greeted their mates with elaborate and exuberant dances, especially after long separations of several months, eager to see each other. In their greeting dances, vital information was communicated about what had been discovered during their separations, passing on pertinent information to family and community. Herons joined crowded colonies, packed full of parents and chicks noisily squawking, eating, and interacting. A single tree could hold dozens of nests where herons voraciously socialized, as this was a survival behavior to keep predators away from their young.

And then, a few months later, each heron flew off to be alone for weeks or months.

As an introvert, as well as a survivor of trauma and violence, I found encouragement from herons to be unafraid of my long stretches of alone time because I knew that in other seasons of my life, I, too, would return to closer relationships and community.

The Role of Harbinger

In their solitary times, herons explored, rested, loafed, and preened themselves for hours. They particularly served as harbingers for their communities, solitarily venturing out to the edges of their habitats to scout, observe, and spot potential shelters and food sources for their next opportunities. Herons took turns being harbingers for their heronries, serving an important role in the survival of their species by establishing the farthest boundaries for their safety.

According to the *Oxford Dictionary*, a harbinger is "a person or thing that announces or signals the approach of something." In Old French, a harbinger ("herberger") was the one who created shelter for protection, often an outpost for the defending army. In a sense, a harbinger was a person who could see what was coming before the others and would protect or warn others. Harbingers went to the edge of what was known, or entered the liminal times between one thing and another, such as the twilight or dawn between day and night to see what was transforming—before it was formed. Moments of awe during my heron walks allowed me to step into these liminal times with a harbinger-like mindset where I could get a glimpse of things before I even understood them. I followed herons to the water's edge, the edges of piers, the edges of rocks, and even the edges of daylight and moonlight.

Fascinated by this harbinger role of herons, I studied how the Egyptians had worshiped a kind of heron, the Bennu, a bird that flew across the Nile into the rising sun, beyond the everlasting light into the afterlife. Revered for embodying the relationship between birth, death, and rebirth, the Bennu is believed to have inspired the Greeks in their fascination with the phoenix. This bird came and went beyond the veil of daylight into vast, wider worlds and served as a messenger of transformation and renewal.

When I saw herons standing alone on the farthest edges of land on long peninsulas, I identified with their solitary role to see what was coming before the others. Perhaps someday my human relationships could benefit from the harbinger role of my alone times. I could show others how to trust the liminal times of their lives and how to grasp new perspectives, unencumbered by the influences of society.

However, in our culture, being alone for long periods could mean isolating and withdrawing from the companionship we were supposed to need. Certainly, my therapists had warned me not to escape from people. But they didn't understand that coming and going from human interaction was a natural way to strengthen our harbinger abilities. The herons convinced me that introverts, creatives, or outliers could learn to serve as harbingers with their insights, wider perspectives, and deeper reflections. Certainly, our greatest writers had spent time alone as harbingers of many different sorts—visionaries, trailblazers, seers. I had read Thoreau's writings, poets such as William Blake, Emily Dickinson, or Rumi, ecologists such as Rachel Carson, and mystics such as Francis of Assisi, as well as others in their solitary vision quests, pilgrimages, and lone adventures. Many of them had endured immense trauma and loss and had found healing in their harbinger experiences—by going to the edge.

In short, harbingers can contribute their insight to others and bring meaning and purpose to their own lives. Trauma survivors can especially find resilience through their own harbinger role.

The Importance of Cleansing and Releasing Toxins

I discovered that the long preening periods of herons, for several hours a day, were not just luxurious pastimes but were essential to their survival. When they preened themselves with their long, sharp beaks, they removed debris, oils, grime, and toxic residue from their skin and feathers, so that their pores were clean and clear. This deep, thorough cleansing allowed their skin's sensing receptors to work more acutely, keenly, and responsively to their environment. Also, I had read that when herons use their beaks to preen their skin and pores, a fine powdery substance is scraped off their skin that serves as a kind of solvent to help absorb the oils that otherwise clogged their pores. Essentially, unclogged and clear pores enhanced the heron's instincts and sharpened their sensory systems, enabling the bird to adapt and maneuver in times of threat.

I thought about the cleaning and preening practices of herons and reflected on how, for me, with my sensitive, thin-skinned nature, I needed to attend to the toxic buildup of residue from my environment. Cleansing, releasing, and purifying were important for highly empathic types like me who tended to take on the energies and moods of people around us. I needed to take seriously the conscious removal of residue that interfered with my emotions, my senses, my intuition, or my instincts. Bathing, steaming, washing, soaking, and rinsing, as well as massage, herbs, and energetic cleansing, were not just pampering pastimes but were all vital to my survival.

Dignity and Grace

Entranced while watching a dance between two herons in courtship, slowly lifting their heads with their long slender necks and mirroring each other in parallel swaying, I instinctively lifted my head and lengthened my neck. Holding my head high, I became tall and elegant. My body could take up more space as I expanded my chest and breathed easily. I walked effortlessly and lightly along the river with the grace of the dancing pair of herons, my arms as free as wings.

I gradually recovered my natural grace from the hunched, tight body I had lived in for over twenty years. I discovered the relationship between grace and dignity as the shame and awkwardness I had carried for so long disappeared from my shoulders and neck. That inner demon that clutched at my throat loosened his grip when I beheld the grace of a circling hawk, osprey, or heron soaring overhead. Gazing upon their sheer elegance, I sensed the dignity within me.

Just by taking the time to be graceful, in the beauty of the moment, my dignity returned.

Beholding and Attunement

Not only was I enchanted by the courtship dances of the heron pairs, but I became entranced by their enchantment with *each other*. Beholding each other, intensely gazing, attuned, and rapturously synchronized in their tiniest movements, they held each other's full attention as exact mirrors of each other, their feathers barely touching, delicately in step and in touch.

Their ability to behold each other, to sway their long necks towards or away from the other, lifting and closing their wings in keen attention, beckoned me to behold their world through their eyes. The blazing slant of the setting sun soaring across my body and across their wings allowed me to behold the wider glow that embraced everything around us. Beholding meant reverence.

When I returned home after my walks, I ritualistically resorted to the *Oxford Dictionary* to understand the words that came to me when I spent time with the herons. I especially loved the root meaning of the word "behold." Derived from Old English *bi* (thoroughly) and *halden* (to hold), it signified to "hold thoroughly."

I let that exquisite word sink in and sighed at the thought that I was so fortunate to be able to "hold thoroughly" the beauty around me by the magic of beholding.

My Blue Notebook

In a slim blue spiral notebook, I wrote down what I learned from my sanctuary times with the herons. I journaled in the evenings after my walks to hold on to the extraordinary array of feelings evoked by the sacred moments of my wildlife encounters. By chronicling and keeping a log of my observations, as well as the responses of my body, mind, and spirit, I was able to spot patterns of synchronicity and divine timing (being at the right place at the right time) in my healing from trauma. Journaling wasn't just an expressive hobby of collecting my essays and poems, or for ranting or venting my anguish, pain, or confusion. Far more than that, journaling was essential to deciphering and understanding my authentic self through my soul's voice as she emerged beyond the ruminations, racing thoughts, and noisy static of my traumatized brain. Mercifully, this voice inside me encouraged my rituals of heron walks that soothed my battered and shell-shocked nervous system.

While writing my reflections, I trusted the same voice that had once stopped me to notice the heron so close to me when I was about to overdose on Valium. This soulful voice that had saved my life offered me simple messages as wise guidelines to live by. I could hear the voice gently saying the word "keepsakes" for keeping myself grounded and remaining in touch with my soul's guidance. Here are the guidelines of my soul's voice that I lived by:

- Keep learning from the herons and the ways of the river.
- Keep writing in your notebook.
- Keep your life simple.
- Keep cleaning houses for work.
- Keep quiet with people—no need to explain yourself.

These guidelines (keepsakes) for myself made me resilient while living with my PTSD symptoms, particularly on the mornings after the nightmares. These promises I made to myself kept me alive.

After two years of many solitary river walks, after cleaning many houses and studios, and filling four notebooks with essays, poems, and ponderous musings, I wondered if I might share my writing with my housecleaning client, Jill, who had become my friend. On Friday evenings, after I'd cleaned her house and she'd come home from work, we occasionally sat at her kitchen table. She loved birds as much as I did, and because our grandmothers both adored chickadees, she eagerly shared her sketchbooks full of songbirds.

One cold, rainy evening, hesitant to walk home, I lingered a bit longer when Jill offered me a cup of Celestial Seasonings cinnamon tea. Her hand rested on her forehead over her brown, wavy hair above her kind eyes, as she thoughtfully listened to me express my admiration for her scarf, turquoise pendant, and bangles.

"Thank you. Oh—I have some birds to show you." She stood up and hurried to find her sketchpad and flipped it open. I spotted little scribbles of notes on the pages near her sparrow and chickadee drawings. She added, "I write down some things about the birds, so I don't forget how they make me feel."

I told her how glad I was that she had saved her drawings and thoughts. "These little notes are like keepsakes. I call these writings and sketches that we save our *keepsakes of the soul*. I believe these things we save really *do* save us."

"Keepsakes . . . I like that word." Jill pondered.

"Would you like to hear one of my keepsakes—one of my poems?" I could hardly believe I was brave enough to offer this.

"Yes, please go ahead," she nodded.

"Here is a short one." I reached for my blue notebook, fumbling through my large canvas tote. I opened it to the right page to read out loud my poem about patience and divine timing that the herons had taught me:

Promises are made with empty hands.
Prayers are made with empty hands.
I watch the herons with empty hands.
Until I hold the hand of someone else.

"Wow, what inspired you to write that?" Jill asked. Reassured by her response, I told her a little about my walks by the river and how the herons taught me life lessons.

"What is it about wild birds that make us feel so hopeful?" Jill wondered. "Amazing how a bird will suddenly show up when we are in trouble or when we need a sign."

"It's the timing of how they show up that fascinates me." I added.

"I believe my grandmother is chatting with me through the chickadees. Somehow, I feel her presence in nature. I haven't told anyone that before." Jill looked at me imploringly, as if seeking validation. "I mean, do you think it's true that we're all connected between species, between generations, to the afterlife?"

"I think so," I humbly replied.

Jill and I delved into a long, fulfilling spiritual conversation. I enjoyed her wondrous, curious mind, and she appreciated the opportunity to deeply explore her beliefs.

"I don't get a chance too often to talk to people this way. You've heard some miraculous things that most people would scoff at as magical thinking. But I trust you—you're open-minded."

I was heartened to hear this. Her encouraging words spurred me to invite her for a walk with me in my river sanctuary, and she accepted my invitation.

A week later, I shared my sacred places by the river with Jill on a long walk, mostly in silence and in wonder. Easily and slowly, we walked, thoughtfully watching chickadees, finches, crows, and geese. The herons did not appear that afternoon, but that was fine as I was relieved by Jill's quiet awe and joy.

I could see her reverence for the wonders of my sanctuary as she wiped away a few tears, standing still in the breeze, beholding two chattering chickadees bouncing at the end of a slender branch.

"They really love it here, don't they?" she smiled sweetly. And then she turned to me and said, "Thank you for taking me here."

"My pleasure," I answered.

And I truly meant it. I genuinely wanted to share my river sanctuary with Jill. After two years of learning to trust my soul's voice through the ways of the herons in their private, protected providence, I knew it was time to show my hidden, glorious world to a friend.

3

Finding Peace Through Wonder

Everything has its wonders, even darkness and silence, and I learn, whatever state I may be in, therein to be content.
—HELEN KELLER, *THE STORY OF MY LIFE*

Building on Strengths

In the early 1980s, I landed a job with one of Jill's friends, a jewelry designer. I joined five other artisans located in a cavernous, toasty basement studio in the old Fan District of Richmond. I learned to polish and file metals, set gemstones, string beads, paint, trim, lacquer, and many other delicate tasks. This hands-on work was grounding and rewarding and provided cozy moments over coffee, between our tasks, to socialize. I felt welcomed and accepted, even though I was told I appeared "a little uptight" and that I needed to chill. Still, in my own awkward way, I enjoyed gallery showings and parties with fellow creative, nerdy, and unconventional types who seemed less judgmental than people in most workplaces.

On gorgeous fall Saturdays, I drove Jill and my new friends to my river sanctuary on the James River for picnics after I bought my first car, a huge dented, used Buick station wagon affectionately named Hank the Tank. Up to six people and a golden lab could pile into Hank along with two guitars, a cooler full of root beers and Miller beers, and a basket of chips, Cheez-Its, and bologna sandwiches. We spread out across blankets in the shade of sycamore trees, played Frisbee with our scampering lab, sang Jimmy Buffet and Queen hits, and bitched and joked about Ronald Reagan, Madonna, and Pee-wee Herman.

Working with artists and still cleaning houses, I saved enough money to take classes for my Bachelor of Fine Arts program at Virginia Commonwealth University. Having studied dance and theater in my childhood and teens, and because I felt comfortable with children (less intimidating than adults), I completed my degree in theater with a minor in dance. Soon I was teaching classes for an after-school arts program called SPARC (School of the Performing Arts in the Richmond Community) in a faculty position that lasted seven years.

I also taught expressive arts classes for children with intellectual and developmental disabilities and eventually went to Scotland to teach for a year at the Craigmillar Festival Society. In these years, working with children and youth with disabilities, in different cultures, often in disadvantaged neighborhoods, I recognized the individual strengths of children that made them resilient. Through the arts, with a strengths-based approach, I was able to engage marginalized groups and break through stigma and shame. Music, dance, and acting were the playful building blocks for finding common ground, creating a safe place, and learning from one another.

I later returned to Virginia Commonwealth University to become a rehabilitation counselor and received my Master of Science degree. With this degree, I could apply all my knowledge of working with children with disabilities. This was a wise and timely choice because I discovered how much the fields of counseling and psychotherapy had changed since I'd been a client ten years earlier. I was heartened to learn about the exciting advances of the recovery model, developed and promoted by the field of rehabilitation counseling, founded on building on the strengths of individuals. The older, well-established medical model, by comparison, was less concerned with the personal strengths of the individual and more focused on treating the diagnosis.

In the 1990s, the field of mental health care was working to remove stigma and emphasis on pathology. Trauma-informed care was on the horizon, fitting well with the new recovery-oriented approaches.

According to SAMHSA (Substance Abuse and Mental Health Services Administration), recovery-oriented care stood apart from the medical model in these fundamental ways[1]:

- Person-centered instead of illness-centered
- Client-driven instead of professionally driven
- Strengths-based instead of deficits-based

Back in 1979, in acute distress, I had sorely needed a person-centered, strengths-based approach when I reached out to clinicians. Disastrously, at that time, I had tried to share the ways I found strength in my heron sanctuaries, on river walks, writing in my journal, and most of all, through my sense of wonder. But they were more interested in fixing my defects than supporting me through my strengths.

They couldn't see that through my sense of wonder, my inner voice could break through the din of rumination and self-loathing. That through my awe-filled reflections with herons in my journal, I found guidance on how to live in balance and well-being. And through my wonder of birds, I found friendship with Jill.

They couldn't see that my sense of wonder had saved my life.

I felt called to enter the rehabilitation counseling field to help other survivors of trauma and loss heal through their strengths that were too often undervalued in the mental health profession, let alone throughout our society. I was driven to make mental health care more empowering (let alone safer) for survivors as well as for people with disabilities. I wanted to advocate for vulnerable people to uphold their rights, strengths, and their personal paths to resilience. I certainly understood how building on strengths, first and foremost, could establish a foundation for eventually reaching beyond our comfort zones to learn new skills and habits (such as how to set boundaries).

I learned in the early 1990s after graduate school as a counselor at a cancer rehabilitation center that people with HIV-AIDS, and those struggling with substance use, needed my *belief* in their personal resilience (not only my recognition). I helped them break through stigma that hindered their trust in professionals as well as themselves. People needed a companionable way to heal themselves with providers, sharing the progress of their strengths and inner guidance that led them to wellness and spiritual growth.

As much as I believed in expertise, rigorous training, and educational standards for professionals, it was essential that the people they served had an equal voice in the process. Certainly, professionals offered guidance and knowledge, but the real healing happened through the *interactions* between clinician and client. I further studied the relational/cultural model of the Jean Baker Miller Institute that valued mutual empathy between the therapist and client, working to reduce the authoritative barriers to building rapport. It was a relief to validate how counselors could use their own empathy—and the language of empathy—to build trust and connection.

The Luna Moth and the Butterfly

It was a blessing that I had my education, my profession, and my sense of purpose to hold onto because I took an enormous leap of faith with a man with whom I fell deeply in love. Of our twelve-year relationship, we were married for ten years. After my disastrous ordeal with domestic violence in my first relationship seven years earlier, I longed to wholeheartedly love someone again, to be intimate, trusting, vulnerable, and strong.

But our marriage broke under the strain of many forces, one of which was my medical condition of premature ovarian failure. I couldn't have children, as I was already post-menopausal at age thirty-five, and for many other painful reasons, my husband and I decided not to adopt a child. I struggled to accept my post-menopausal body—and the loss of my sense of womanhood and youth. Five years younger than me, my husband felt powerless in supporting me through this raw, barren sense of loss. Therapy could not save our marriage, and worse, the therapist may have ruined my fragile confidence in ever being a mother. He calmly and resolutely announced, in front of my husband, "You need to work more on your trauma issues before you adopt a child." I felt the sting of being deemed defective, though I bravely proclaimed to my husband and therapist that I would bring my compassion and wisdom to being a mother and a wife, despite surviving decades of trauma. But my husband was in doubt, and I will forever believe that this therapist gave my husband cold feet about raising a child with me.

One gloomy Sunday afternoon, after we had reached a bitter point in a circular conversation about separating from our marriage, I drove to the river for a long walk, while he raked and weeded in our garden. In those three hours apart, as I sauntered along the leafy paths by the water, I spotted the shell of a luna moth and delicately picked up her beautiful green body. The luminescence of her wings took my breath away, although she was dead. I sobbed a little, for her beauty as well as for her death, and for my own sorrow. I couldn't just leave her winged body there on the ground. I carefully placed her in tissues and softly carried her home in my handbag.

At home, I showed her to my husband, displaying her brilliant emerald body on our kitchen counter. My husband, amazed, grabbed my arm in excitement, and we both stood still. And then, to my utter surprise, he proclaimed, "You're not gonna believe this—I found a monarch butterfly this afternoon! Let me show you." He rushed back to our porch and carried the shell of this butterfly up to me, holding it carefully in the palms of his hands, and then laying it down on the counter next to my luna moth.

There they were, the luna moth and the monarch butterfly, lying together for us to adore. We paused again in awe and wonderment.

"When did you find your moth?" he asked.

"About 2:30," I answered.

"Holy shit, that's when I found my monarch."

"Wow—just totally incredible. The perfect timing is amazing," I exclaimed.

"Do you think it's a sign of something?"

"It must be, but I'm not quite sure what it means," I pondered.

He sat down on our wicker couch and held out his arms for me to come join him. I eagerly sat next to him, and he put his arm around me. Our tuxedo cat, Ivan, jumped up near us, purring, and I quietly stroked his fur. The three of us sat together like a family while we listened to the rain falling softly outside. A moist breeze drifted through the screen door as Ivan licked his paws. Another stronger breeze pushed through the screen, blowing an empty paper cup off the kitchen table and rolling it around the floor. Ivan watched the cup but stayed with us on the couch.

After a long, pensive silence, my husband sighed. "I love your sense of wonder, Val."

I turned to him. "I never knew that. . . . I'm glad to know that. You marvel at things too. I love that about you."

For all the disappointment in our lives and in each other, during our last year of marriage, we shared our love through brief moments of wonder. We added time for more evening walks and traveled often to the Maine coast. We listened to awe-inspiring music by the mystical saint Hildegard von Bingen, and the exquisite performances of Celtic Woman, many Windham Hill artists, and Gregorian chants. We read wondrous poems by Mary Oliver, Robert Bly, and Native American poet Joy Harjo. We saw *Riverdance* performed live, astounding us as we sat in a huge audience.

Perhaps our luna moth and butterfly experience represented transformation—and accepting change. We were not the same people we thought we had married, and we had drifted into loneliness. Yet on Sundays, we shared our more soulful selves, including our writing. We read to each other from our journals and projects. It was my husband who most believed in me as a writer, and even on the day we separated, he encouraged me never to give up. I will always be grateful to him for that.

The grief of our divorce and not being able to have children was so profound that I ached to leave everything behind in Richmond. It was time to break ties with the past. I longed to move to a more remote and wilder part of the United States, the coast of Maine—a whole different watery world where I knew herons thrived.

Maine

I arrived in Yarmouth, Maine, in April 2000, with a car full of small wicker furniture, boxes of books, binders, watercolors, and delicately wrapped feathers, crystals, teapots, and cups. Ivan, my aging cat, a remarkably adaptable companion, was happy to step out of his carrier into my tiny studio apartment, quickly spotting his litter box that I had just placed in the bathroom.

We loved our cozy home tucked at the back of a restored sea captain's house next to an apple orchard. We each sat in our own wicker chair by a wide window where the sun poured over us as I sipped my French roast coffee.

I joined in Ivan's joys through his daily habits and routines, such as ceremoniously giving him his shrimp treats and throwing his catnip toys across unpacked boxes, laundry baskets, and hallways for him to run and fetch. He curled up with me under a blanket while I imagined the books I would write someday and listened to me espouse out loud my new lease on life. He sat on my desk watching me cry over emails from my ex-husband after hearing he had remarried and that a child was on the way. I held Ivan at night while lying in bed, gazing at the stars through the skylight window above us.

We even had a ritual of taking our blood pressure medicine together at bedtime because Ivan's vet prescribed Atenolol, which was exactly what my doctor prescribed for me. Despite his hypertrophic heart condition, he reached the grand old age of eighteen a few years later.

Maine was ideal for me, a place for introverts, individualists, quiet introspection, and personal healing. I was not seeking a social life, which was fortunate, as this rural, northern stretch of New England was inhabited by reserved and private people for the most part. As a Southerner from Virginia, I had to adjust to the brisker, less effusive tone and ditch the perfunctory small talk I had been raised to politely offer. Here it was considered more polite to talk less and mind your own business. And that was fine with me—a welcome change.

I worked as a case manager four days a week at a mental health agency, which allowed three days off to explore the vast coastline and islands of the Gulf of Maine. On these treasured days, I flourished in glorious solitude, practically living a monastic existence. I soon discovered Wolfe's Neck Woods State Park on the Harraseeket River near Freeport and marveled at the large population of blue herons, egrets, ospreys, ducks, owls, chickadees, and much more. I roamed and wandered through dense forests of tall pines, over windswept hillsides, and out onto long peninsulas at low tide. I rested on sunny patches of moss and grass between the rocks, gazing out across the bay to many tiny islands, such as Googins Island.

One day I saw seventeen herons wading in the water. How they thrived throughout Casco Bay! I had read that the Abenaki Native tribe had named this bay Aucocisco, meaning "place of herons." I loved the thought that this place that I now called home had been a paradise for herons for many hundreds, if not thousands of years.

A gust of wind grabbed my attention, and I heard a chickadee singing nearby. I stood up and stepped towards the pine tree where I could clearly see the bold little bird chatting at the top of its lungs. It flew towards me and landed right on my head! I paused and stood still as I held my breath and felt the breathing of this tiny body. Time stopped. Everything stopped, except for the little breaths of the feathered creature on my head. Then, amazingly, the chickadee gently tapped its beak twice on my forehead! It felt like a kiss. Seconds later, as if the mission had been completed by my winged visitor, it just flew off, rising higher to a branch on the next pine tree.

I was so stunned by this miraculous encounter that I sat down on a tree stump and stared out to the glistening blue bay. I couldn't help but wonder if this chickadee kiss was sent by Viv, who had adored these birds. Why had this chickadee visited me in such a bold, fearless way?

A wave of love warmed my heart as a few tears of gratitude trickled down my face. I basked in this sweet, wondrous moment, feeling blessed by this freely given gift with no strings attached, just a fleeting, glorious rush of love. "Thank you, Viv." I couldn't help but speak out loud.

To my surprise, while remembering Viv and savoring this chickadee encounter, I could hear her voice whispering, "Your father would love this place." Her message alarmed me. Yes, I agreed with her that my father would love the beauty of this place. But dare I bring him here?

I wondered about my father visiting me in Maine. I had hardly seen him for twenty years since my parents had divorced. Once I'd run to Florida to stay with him for shelter during the time I was trying to escape my perpetrator, but that visit had ended disastrously. I was semi-estranged from him and carefully chose the times I could handle a visit.

His mood could shift in seconds at the slightest glance. His volatility was triggered by any sign of vulnerability shown by anyone, especially by his children. We had to be pleasant—or else. And yet a playful side of him encouraged long rounds of imaginative storytelling after dinner, particularly around my grandmother's wide oak table.

He loved photography, birds, and light—especially light: sunrises, rays of light, candlelight, golden light, light from prisms and rainbows, northern lights, starlight, moonlight, auras, tiny sparkles on dew. He taught me to see the beauty and light in all things, although I had to be careful not to share too much of the light of my spirit with him. He was tormented, but he revered the marvels of art and nature. I often imagined him as an elegant and eccentric Oscar-winning cinematographer instead of slogging through decades of selling computer hardware as an account executive. Something in this brilliantly artistic and romantic man had been so broken early in his life. There were fragments of exquisite giftedness mixed in among the cracked pieces and parts of his personality that never fit together.

Growing up as a military brat during the Second World War, he moved all over the world with his mother and sister, following his father, an admiral commanding ships in the Pacific. He was taken from California to Virginia to Hawaii to California to Italy after the war, and back to Virginia—all by the age of sixteen. He never had a solid sense of himself, let alone a childhood, as he was the "little man of the house," who took the punishments for the family when his father came home on leave. He became a kid shapeshifter, a remarkably adaptable, if not charming, companion for his ever-changing world of friends, classmates, neighbors, or relatives he met during the war years.

Fortunately, recently, he had been in therapy and was now somewhat better able to regulate his emotions. He had even sent me a plaintive email apologizing for his abusive behavior. He worked hard to improve himself, reaching out to his adult children while facing long, lonely stretches of grief after his second wife had died of early-onset Alzheimer's.

Should I ever allow him to visit me—here on the coast of Maine, my home far away from my past? Was I strong enough for that? I held off deciding this for several months until my birthday in October when he called and asked if I would like to see him. He told me he had taken many photographs in Maine last year when traveling with a friend further up the coast in Blue Hill.

I knew I could entertain him by showing him the coastal beauty of my town, but could I spend a few hours with *him*? That evening, I tapped into my gut feelings. It struck me that when he had his camera outdoors, he was calm and serene.

I decided to allow a visit—as long as he brought his camera.

We met at a nearby restaurant in Freeport for an early breakfast of blueberry pancakes and eggs, and planned our walk to Wolfe's Neck Woods. He had his camera. He appeared respectful, attentive, and a little nervous as I carefully and tensely shared interesting factoids, trivia, and news about the towns on Casco Bay.

Maybe I was lucky, maybe it was his camera, or maybe it was a miracle—but my father was quietly fascinated when we arrived at my sanctuary of herons. In the shallow waters at low tide, two herons stood still and didn't mind us at all. In silence, almost reverently, he took photographs of herons, of me, of rocks, and of the sea. We walked further along the narrow coastal path between hundreds of tall, giant pines and stopped at wide tidal pools and little sun-soaked beaches surrounded by goldenrods. Delighted and smiling, he frequently paused to take photos until we finally sat on a fallen tree.

A hawk soared overhead.

"Look—did you see that?" my father asked, astonished.

"Yes, I sure did—a hawk!"

"You know, Val, I never told you how much I love red-tailed hawks."

I listened closely.

"Hawks are to me like herons are to you."

"I never knew that about you," I admitted, surprised.

"The greatest peace I've ever felt was when I saw a red-tail early one morning while I was sitting on my balcony. The sun was coming up through the branches and this hawk just sat there. Right there, staring at me... took my breath away. It sounds so simple, but I've never been the same since that morning."

After a pause, taking in his words, I nodded slowly. "The herons bring me peace, too."

He tenderly smiled at me. "I'm glad to know that. It means a lot to me to hear that." His words came as a profound relief. We could understand each other after all. We didn't have much more to say, but we welcomed our silence as we walked back through the long slant of light between the pines and along the shore of the shimmering bay.

When we drove back to Freeport, my father surprised me by suddenly offering to buy me a birthday present. He thought I could use a set of binoculars so I could watch my herons more closely. We enjoyed our time at the L.L. Bean outlet store, where he bought himself a rain jacket and a sturdy set of binoculars for me.

He never made it back to Maine, but I visited him four more times in Virginia before he died from a series of strokes. At least he knew the peace of a moment of acceptance and serenity we had shared on that October morning in my sanctuary of herons.

Note

1 Chiu, M. Y., Ho, W. W., Lo, W. T., & Yiu, M. G. (2010). Operationalization of the SAMHSA model of recovery: A quality of life perspective. *Quality of Life Research: An International Journal of Quality of Life Aspects of Treatment, Care and Rehabilitation, 19*(1), 1–13. https://doi.org/10.1007/s11136-009-9555-2.

4

Reclaiming My Sense of Wonder

The invariable mark of wisdom is to see the miraculous in the common.
—RALPH WALDO EMERSON, *NATURE*

My Little Book of Wonders

Fast approaching my sixties, I relocated to the Boston area from Maine in 2013 in search of a stronger support system and better-paying jobs. My quiet, tranquil life in Maine had become too reclusive and limited as an older single woman. Proud of my new life in Boston, I proactively built a social life as well as a small business teaching poetry and wordplay classes at senior centers and mentoring young adults with developmental disabilities. I treasured my wide network of colleagues, friends, and clients, as well as a sense of community and walkability in the city and nearby towns.

Indeed, I was so confident and pleased with my new life that I began blogging for *Psychology Today* on the topic of building a social life, and I wrote a book about starting over and finding community called *400 Friends and No One to Call*, published in March 2020.

But March 2020 was also when the Covid-19 pandemic struck the world and destroyed much of everything I had built—including the successful launch of my book. Living alone at age sixty-five, financially strapped, without my classes and clients to teach in person, and with no income from my book sales, I worried about how I would survive. On top of this, I was already in deep debt and had maxed out my credit cards from tackling thyroid cancer a few months before Covid hit (although the carcinoma was caught in the early stages, the bills were frighteningly high). I took early Social Security retirement benefits and taught a few classes through Zoom, but most of my business was lost. I could hardly pay rent and waited in lines at two food pantries every week.

I took solitary strolls along the grassy trails of the Assabet River near my home in the town of Maynard. I longed for the solace I had always found on my river walks. The goldenrod grew plentifully along the breezy path, but now I hardly felt the glow in my heart that I had once enjoyed on my long walks in Maine or Virginia. I could spot a blue heron circling overhead, or a chickadee darting from pine to pine, but I only observed halfheartedly as if watching a screen, detached from my senses. My all-consuming thoughts separated my heart and soul from the vibrant life around me. It seemed I had lost my reverence for the natural world—and even the wonder of my beloved herons.

It wasn't only the hard grip of survival mode that kept me from enjoying the wildlife around me. A haunting sense of loneliness that

I was no longer essential in anyone's life kept me from believing I belonged anywhere, not even in the natural world. I ruminated on my disconnection from people, as well as from wildlife.

During the pandemic, it seemed I was always the person initiating the check-in calls, the friendly emails, the Zooms, the Spotify playlists, and the podcast recommendations. Hardly any friend or colleague had read my book. (Could anything be lonelier than writing a book about loneliness and no one reading it?) Keeping in touch with people required too much effort, and I was tired of doing all the reaching out. I was fed up with being ghosted, strung along, and having no one get back to me. On top of all that, I had not been touched by a single human being for six months—and my body was truly "touch starved."

The next two years dragged on as I struggled through major depression. Though I slowly began teaching more classes for seniors through Zoom and wearing masks to work with my fragile clients, my social life and business had still not been restored to pre-pandemic levels. I hardly ever saw my friends or colleagues in person anymore. The collective mood of the US was distrustful, testy, and tense, and I generally preferred to stay home, brood, and write alarming articles about ghosting and loneliness for *Psychology Today*.

Because my landlord suddenly had to sell the property I was renting, I moved three different times between 2021 and 2022. I rented drafty, semi-furnished rooms month-to-month, schlepping my belongings around in my old 2009 Toyota Matrix, and stuffing my duffle bags into musty closets. I ended up moving in with a roommate I had met through Craigslist to a small, sunny apartment in West Roxbury, a pleasant, safe, and lively neighborhood in Boston.

One day in April, unpacking my boxes of keepsakes, I rediscovered my old journals from 1979 and the early 1980s. To my surprise, lying under those notebooks was a little book I had written long ago at the age of twelve, in 1968, titled "Wonder and Dreams." I had not read this sweet collection of poems and reflections for thirty years. Although I had saved this delicate book made of marbled paper as a charming memento and carried it with me wherever I lived, I had hardly appreciated the words so carefully handwritten alongside my tiny drawings.

I sat down by the window to enjoy this little forgotten treasure. My twelve-year-old self had written words expressing pure enchantment in a language fluid in wonder and awe, full of praises, blessings, wishes, and ponderous musings. I read tales of climbing oak trees under the stars, gathering watercress in bubbling streams for my grandmother, listening to accordions playing in a local Italian restaurant, dancing in my toe shoes, and watching kittens being born—all true in glorious detail. This book I held was truly a book of wonders, and reading it did indeed restore my sense of wonder.

I gazed through the window onto the tall old oak trees glistening after a rain shower. It struck me that my capacity to be wondrous, amazed, and touched by the world around me had prevailed at the core of my being throughout my life. As a child, my father had even given me a nickname, "Wowinda," because I said "wow" so often! On our walk at Wolfe's Neck Woods, decades later, I realized he admired that quality in me—or perhaps he loved me for it.

Reflecting on my little book of wonders, I realized my wonder and awe didn't always need to come from my encounters with blue herons, chickadees, or river walks, or from wildlife at all. My moments of awe didn't need to rely on any *particular* source. Instead, more fundamentally, it was my willingness to be amazed, my openness, and my love of beholding the wonders around me that had made me resilient. Awe and wonder didn't only come from my love of blue herons.

I wondered about other sources of awe in my life.

Nature, dreams, poetry, literature, music, art, dance, cats, dogs, legends, mysteries, telepathy, intuition, synchronicity, divine timing, writings from saints and mystics, acts of heroism by humans, brilliant discoveries by scientists, athletic feats, crowds of thousands showing up for social change or inspiration, miracles, cancer going into remission, childbirth, unconditional love, the human spirit living through trauma and loss . . .

I realized this list was endless! I was often in awe of things, great or tiny, fleeting or everlasting, sudden or gradual, brief or constant, vast or intricate, nuanced or bold.

I basked in my breakthrough that my sense of wonder had been a source of strength *all* my life, not only a coping mechanism for trauma or an escape from pain. This was an innate quality in me that I could claim as a foundation of my resilience as well as my character.

Thanks to my little book of wonders that I had written fifty years earlier, I claimed my sense of wonder as my birthright. It came naturally, easily. And I could always count on it. Unlike the uncertain and unreliable success of my business, my relationships, my writing, and the unpredictability of the world, I could always turn to my sense of wonder, at least for a moment of beauty. Even a fleeting, brief encounter with something wondrous, such as spotting the moon rising over the rooftops, my ability to be amazed was a constant source of strength inside me, always there to be tapped.

This thought reminded me of what Rachel Carson said in her book *Silent Spring*: "Those who contemplate the beauty of the earth find reserves of strength that will endure for as long as life lasts."

I reflected on her words that through our wonder of the beauty around us we can find enduring reserves of strength. These words rang particularly true for me as a survivor of trauma and loss. Inspired by her wisdom that wonder was a source of strength, I began reading her books *Silent Spring* and *The Sense of Wonder*. I was especially moved by her writings about the importance of teaching children how to develop their sense of wonder and how vital this ability is, not only for the survival of our earth but for the preservation of our humanity. "The more clearly we can focus our attention on the wonders and realities of the universe around us, the less taste we shall have for destruction."

Especially as a survivor of trauma, I found meaning in her words that our sense of wonder was a way of preventing ourselves from destructive habits or behaviors, in *ourselves* as well as in our society. If, as she prescribed in *The Sense of Wonder*, we taught ourselves and others to see our natural world through wonder and awe, we could preserve the best of our true nature as well as the best of humanity.

Certainly, through my moments of awe and wonder with my friend Jill, with my grandmother Viv, and even with my father, I had seen the best of them in a whole new light. Our shared experiences of awe brought out the best in us. And reflecting on my little book written when I was twelve, looking back through my childhood's pure sense of wonder, I saw the best in myself—my openness, curiosity, and love of life.

Discovering the Neuroscience of Awe and Wonder

Thanks to my discovery of Rachel Carson's writing about wonder as a source of strength, and because she appreciated wonder as a scientist, I began to explore awe and wonder through the wide, fascinating frontier of neuroscience. Recently, neuroscience has sparked a revolution in our understanding of the underexplored and underappreciated emotions of awe and wonder.

Taking a neuroscientific approach to wonder and awe was entirely new for me. I was well educated on the ways of wonder through the arts, mythology, inspirational and spiritual literature, and depth psychology. I had read exquisitely wondrous poetry (from Mary Oliver, Wendell Berry, or William Blake) and I had devoured books of awe-filled accounts of saints and mystics by Matthew Fox or Andrew Harvey. I was fascinated by *The Varieties of Religious Experience* by William James, and I had studied other contemplative religious works by Thomas Merton and Henri Nouwen. I had read Carl Jung on the topic of synchronicity, *Animal Speak* by Ted Andrews, and *Soul Retrieval* by Sandra Ingerman on healing encounters with totem animals. I adored books on the wondrous aspects of our soul, such as *Anam Cara* by John O'Donohue, *Care of the Soul* by Thomas Moore, or *Women Who Run with the Wolves* by Clarissa Pinkola Estes.

All these works had inspired and encouraged my sense of wonder for decades. Up to now, the world had taught me that wonder and awe were soulful states of mind that we kept sacred or private, for quiet, intimate reflection. Certainly, we could curl up in a secluded spot and enjoy a wonderfully spiritual book of blessings or ecstatically mystical poems. But we had to be careful with whom we shared our wonder. If anything, being awestruck or feeling full of wonder was something akin to being gullible, naïve, or childlike. Indeed, the underappreciated emotions of awe and wonder in previous models of mental health or human development had left me baffled, if not embarrassed, by my highly wonder-seeking nature. Like many other trauma survivors, I was hesitant to share my moments of awe and wonder with most people, keeping these beautiful, inspirational (and often spiritual) encounters very private. These experiences may have seemed too "woo-woo," or "out there" for casual conversation. Others might think we were misguided by magical thinking or by a lack of critical thinking, or whacked out on conspiracy theories or psychic predictions. Or just plain immature.

Given this history of my wonder-seeking nature being misunderstood and underappreciated (or judged), I was fascinated by what neuroscience had to say. To my delight and surprise, I discovered a vast and fast-growing body of research that actually stunned me.

As a blogger for *Psychology Today*, I noticed the topic of awe increasingly trending on the cover pages. I delved into reading articles by popular and well-respected researchers including Dacher Keltner, Michelle Shiota, Jennifer Stellar, Ethan Kross, Alice Chirico, Maria Monroy, David Yaden, and many others. I studied comprehensive research on awe from the Greater Good Science Center and reviewed extensive studies published by the American Psychological Association and the National Institutes of Health.

I was heartened by the ways these researchers were describing awe and wonder and tackling the societal biases that had limited our understanding of these complex emotions. Even the definitions of awe and wonder were being examined and redefined. In *Awe: The New Science of Everyday Wonder and How It Can Transform Your Life*, Dacher Keltner described awe as "the feeling of being in the presence of something vast that transcends your current understanding of the world." [1]

I read many definitions of wonder, including the *Oxford Dictionary* version. Wonder is "a feeling of surprise and admiration, caused by something beautiful, unexpected, or unfamiliar." As a verb, to wonder means "to feel curious or desire to know." Researchers proposed that wonder is often an offshoot of an experience of awe. Dacher Keltner states, "Wonder, the mental state of openness, questioning, curiosity, and embracing mystery, arises out of experiences of awe."[2] We usually wonder about something awesome that happened to us. For example, after an encounter with a blue heron that saved my life, I wandered into river sanctuaries full of herons and spent time basking in wonderment.

Keltner and other researchers such as Alice Chirico and David Yaden describe awe as a self-transcending emotion that allows us to go beyond our self-referential thoughts, our needs, and beyond our own mindset. Essentially, awe can give us a greater, wider perspective to see the bigger picture.

Neuroscience explains how these powerful moments of awe and wonder allow us to see ourselves in a whole new light—a state of awareness beyond our habitual patterns of thinking. Awe grabs our attention away from our self-referential thoughts and pulls us out of our self-absorption. Dacher Keltner has called our sense of self within this expanded, vast perspective our "small self," an awareness of being a small part of a much wider world beyond our own lives. This vast, all-inclusive sense of oneness helps us feel humility and compassion for others around us.

In a BBC article, "Awe: The little earthquake that could free your mind," University of Michigan psychologist Ethan Kross describes awe as "the wonder we feel when we encounter something powerful that we can't easily explain."[3] Awe and wonder leave us speechless and stunned for a moment, a pause—an instant change that resets our thought patterns. Kross adds, "When you are in the presence of something vast and indescribable, you feel smaller, and so does your negative chatter."[4] Kross has conducted studies with PTSD survivors, including military veterans and youth from underserved communities. One study in which participants joined a rafting trip in Utah demonstrated how their feelings of awe predicted better outcomes in their well-being months later.[5] In short, when we experience awe, we turn our attention outwards instead of inwards. We are better able to attune to one another in the moment.

Social psychologist Michelle Shiota, a researcher at Arizona State University, describes how awe helps us break out of our "predictive coding" about what is supposed to happen next. Awe allows us to break out of our expectations, assumptions, and biases about what we think is likely to happen as the experience unfolds. "The mind dials back its 'predictive coding' to just look around and gather information."[6] So awe literally puts reality right in front of us. Our minds practically gasp when we're overcome with awe—we "get it" on some level even if we cannot explain it.

Jennifer Stellar, a psychologist at the University of Toronto, has been studying how awe affects our sense of interconnection, meaning, and purpose. Her studies show how we tend to be more aware of one another after a shared experience of awe when our sense of self diminishes and we see one another in a new light, less influenced by stereotypes and bias.[7] Another benefit of awe that Jennifer Stellar studied was how inflammation in our bodies is reduced through awe experiences that also reduce levels of cortisol due to anxiety and stress responses.[8]

Heartening News for Survivors of Trauma and Loss

For the survivor of trauma and loss, the findings from the extensive research on awe and wonder offer heartening news. Neuroscience demonstrates how states of awe deactivate the mind circuitry that is known as the default mode network (DMN), the parts of our brain that think about ourselves—our self-referential thinking. The DMN is the source of our negative self-talk, ruminations, obsessive thinking, and anticipatory thinking that makes us more likely to be biased about outcomes (projections of outcomes), self-absorbed, and overly self-conscious. Researchers have consistently found that moments of awe deactivate the DMN, which allows us to perceive the world around us in a less anxious, less self-centered, and more objective way.

Based on these discoveries, I could identify the benefits for trauma and loss survivors:

- Even brief moments of awe can shift our attention out of rumination and negative chatter.
- Awe calms our nervous system, shifting us into the parasympathetic response (the opposite of the stress response).
- Awe breaks us out of our predictive coding (anticipation and expectation) in our thought processes of what will happen next—so we are more open to a new experience.

- We feel less alone and separate from the world around us (oneness and belonging to something greater than ourselves).

- We see the big picture with a wider perspective on our lives (small self in the midst of vastness).

- We feel a sense of humility, compassion, and interconnection with others.

These findings on the self-transcending features of awe explained my healing experiences with the blue herons, chickadees, the sanctuaries of bays and rivers, and my wondrous moments with Viv, Jill, and my father. I felt immensely liberated by the neuroscience that revealed remarkable ways these mysterious, intricate, and brilliant emotional states of awe had preserved my well-being and resilience throughout my life.

It was especially enlightening to discover a self-assessment tool for exploring our awe experiences called the Awe Experience Scale.[9] This was created by an international collaboration of psychologists to help us identify and examine six particular features of an awe experience. These six factors of the Awe Experience Scale are:

1. The Perception of Vastness: This can be a physical sense or a perceptual sense of vastness.

2. Need for Accommodation: You might not be able to absorb the experience at once. It is indescribable.

3. Alterations in Time: Time may seem to slow down, stop, or stand still.

4. Self-diminishment (or a sense of the small self): You feel smaller in the presence of so much greatness around you.

5. Connectedness: You feel a sense of oneness or belonging with everything or everyone around you.

6. Physical Sensations: You feel chills, or goosebumps, or you gasp, or freeze, or your jaw drops.

Given these six characteristics of an awe experience, I reexamined my experiences with the blue herons on the river back in 1979. Certainly, these six features of the Awe Experience Scale all matched my powerful healing moments. Reviewing my heron encounters and walks, I could clearly see what was happening to me at those times. In short, activation in all six factors of the Awe Experience Scale had been evident.

Vastness: Yes, in my river sanctuaries I felt liberated wandering through the vast open spaces overlooking the river and the skies. I felt free and open to life around me.

> **Alterations in Time:** A different sense of time was one of the first features I noticed when I was with the herons. Time seemed to stand still. I slowed down and my thoughts settled down. I could pace myself and steady the rhythms of my body, mind, and spirit.
>
> **Self-diminishment (or sense of a small self):** My thoughts that were centered on myself (my rumination and shame) seemed to diminish when I shifted my mind to what was outside of me rather than inside of me. The herons and the beauty of the river lifted my focus out of my head and away from my self-referential thinking—a merciful break from my inner torment.

- **Connectedness:** I felt a sense of oneness, peace, and belonging in my sanctuary of herons. I didn't feel alone or afraid. I felt I had a place there in the providence of this natural world where I belonged with all the water birds.

- **Physical sensations:** I felt chills of awe as well as a warm, radiant glow of peace. My body felt graceful, grounded, and in tune with the grace of the birds. Indeed, this profound sense of grace and peace made me feel dignified and elegant.

- **Need for accommodation:** My experiences were indescribable (blew me away) and sensorily saturating at times. I needed to process these encounters later in my blue notebook with much reflection.

In these states of awe with the herons and my deep attunement to them, I was able to learn life lessons that helped me care for myself, especially my trauma symptoms. My mind was open to observing the wisdom of nature by being receptive to the wildlife around me.

Misconceptions and Realities that Neuroscience Showed Me

What particularly amazed me about the research was that it shone a light on my own biases about awe and wonder (mostly internalized from societal influences). I was shocked to realize that so many common misconceptions had skewed or diminished my ability to experience awe. It was liberating to bust these myths and biases and see the qualities of awe and wonder through the new light of neuroscience.

Here are five realizations that opened my eyes.

Misconception 1

Awe comes more naturally to deep thinkers, artists, or spiritually minded people.

Reality

It is the trait of *openness to experience* that leads to awe in both introverts and extroverts, according to research using the Five-Factor Model of Personality. People who are curious, open-minded, and interested in learning about the world tend to have more experiences of awe. [10]Scientists as well as artists, religious people as well as agnostics, and introspective thinkers as well as enthusiastic travelers all have in common the trait of openness.

For survivors of trauma and loss: Our openness to learning, curiosity, and willingness to see the world through different perspectives gives us the gifts of wonder and awe.

Misconception 2

You need to be in nature to have meaningful or valid moments of awe.

Reality

According to the research of Dacher Keltner, there are eight domains of human experience or "wonders of life" in which we can tap into our sense of wonder and awe. Nature is one path, but we can also find awe through a wide variety of experiences. You could have an immersive, wondrous experience watching a Coldplay concert live among 30,000 people singing "A Sky Full of Stars," or you could marvel at gymnast Simone Biles brilliantly competing at the Paris Olympics. Or you could have an epiphany one morning after a lucid dream. All of these experiences give us moments that take our breath away.

For survivors of trauma and loss: Wonder is accessible to us no matter where we are. It is heartening to remember the ways we have found wonder in more limited environments when we were unable to be outdoors or lacked access to the wilderness.

Misconception 3

To gain the benefits of awe and wonder, you need to have a big, powerful, profound experience.

For example, I once had a powerful experience with a blue heron that transformed my life. I believed for decades that it was my love of herons and the magic of the river that gave me strength. This was true, especially when I was younger, but now I have rediscovered *many* other ways I experience awe that restore myself. Freeing myself from my attachment to having enormously powerful experiences has been a relief to me!

Reality

Small, brief, and frequent experiences of awe and wonder, over time, offer many benefits to our well-being. We can cultivate opportunities for awe and wonder.

Neuroscience features findings that show it is the *frequency* of awe moments that matter, no matter how small or brief. Studies reveal how smaller daily doses of awe and wonder can provide, over time, the greatest benefits to our well-being. Taking an "awe walk" in the early morning on a regular basis can give us an opportunity to open ourselves to awe-inspiring encounters.

For survivors of trauma and loss: Even if anxiety or depression depletes our energy and attention, we can still pause for a moment of awe periodically throughout the day.

Misconception 4

You need to be in a calm, clear state of mind to have an experience of awe.

Many of us believe that if we are upset, ruminating, worried, or overthinking, then we will not be able to have a moment of awe and wonder.

Reality

Sudden, unexpected moments of awe and wonder *do* happen to people who are struggling through grief and trauma. Surprising experiences of awe quickly switch our attention outward and out of the grip of our self-referential thinking.

For survivors of trauma and loss: A moment of awe releases us from the grip of rumination or nagging thoughts and truly gives us a break from our mindset.

Misconception 5

To be wowed, you need to rely on a certain source of awe to excite you.

This means that you can only feel awe in a particular way, such as when you go on vacation to a special place, see your totem bird, join a spiritual retreat, immerse yourself in a huge concert, or be visited by the spirit of a loved one.

Reality

Even though it is healthy to regularly return to sources of awe that restore us, it is helpful to remember that awe often comes to us as a surprise. Unexpectedly, suddenly, and fleetingly, something happens that takes your breath away—and you pause to take it in. Let's say you were on a walk by a lake, hoping for a "sign" from your totem bird, but suddenly a rainbow pops out of the sky and illuminates the water in glorious rays of light. Instead of feeling disappointed that your "sign" did not appear, a rainbow glow is there to enchant you.

For survivors of trauma and loss: It is our willingness to be wowed—not only the thing that wows us—that we can claim as a source of strength.

Sharing Moments of Wonder with Others

Although the years of 2020 to 2022 had been lonely and discouraging as I faced many losses in my business, friendships, finances, and health, I was excited by my rediscovery of awe as a source of resilience, thanks to the validation of neuroscience.

But this sense of hope and inspiration about the healing power of wonder was not only for my own personal benefit. In these uncertain times in our world, with so much loneliness and hopelessness around us, I wanted to reach out to others who could benefit from reclaiming their own wondrous voice within them. In an energizing and joyous surge of mission and vision, I began teaching poetry courses that celebrated wonder at local senior centers and assisted living communities.

My classes were welcomed as my audiences grew, hungry to read and discuss wondrous, mysterious, and life-affirming poetry, especially seniors who had been isolated during the harsher periods of the pandemic. It struck me that my desire to create opportunities for others to share awe was healing in itself. An eighty-year-old woman who was grieving the loss of her husband due to Covid-19 a year earlier was inspired through a wonder-filled poem by Mary Oliver and shared her own story of wonder. Her tender, thoughtful reliving of a memory of an amazing moment with her husband moved the six other participants in the class and sparked them to speak of wondrous experiences. Inspired, I continued more classes that provided healing spaces for sharing moments of awe. Poetry could certainly elicit such states of wonderment that led to storytelling and recollection—and I wondered about the potential healing for survivors of trauma and loss to share their stories in other settings.

I had recently given a talk for a grief support group at an organization called the Sun Will Rise Foundation, based in Braintree, Massachusetts, and had enjoyed a warm and authentic connection with the founder and director, Robyn Houston-Bean. She seemed particularly interested in my work with seniors telling their "wonder stories" and was curious to learn more about the benefits of awe and wonder in helping people live with grief, loss, and major life changes.

Over the next few weeks, Robyn and I delved into amazing conversations about the ways our moments of awe had given us resilience in facing grief, loneliness, and trauma. I shared with her my discoveries from the neuroscience of awe, and we considered the ways we could facilitate healing conversation in our groups. Heartened by our ideas, she aimed to provide a dedicated time in her support groups for members to share stories of awe and wonder. Soon several group members in other recovery and grief support groups offered to tell their stories to appreciative audiences. We were overjoyed that many survivors of grief, addiction, and trauma were willing to come forth with their stories of wonder to be heard, recognized, and celebrated in our groups.

We named our storytelling project "The Healing Through Wonder Project." Through our stories, it struck me that our sense of wonder was more than a source of strength. Wonder was also a source of connection. The meaningful sense of community through sharing wonder with others enriched our healing beyond our expectations—easing us out of isolation. And finally, our sense of connection and community through wonder brought peace of mind to grieving family members who had lost loved ones to overdose or addiction. Even if they might not ever find closure for their loss, and even if the loss was ambiguous and complicated, at least, through experiences of shared awe, they could feel a momentary sense of peace and acceptance.

In short, Robyn and I realized that sharing experiences of awe and wonder with others could build resilience for living with grief, as well as living with uncertainty.

My sense of purpose was renewed by collaborating with Robyn on her grief support groups through our Healing Through Wonder Project, and by teaching my wonder-enhancing poetry classes at several senior centers. I blogged for *Psychology Today* and for *The Health Story Collaborative* about all that I was learning.

In the meantime, to my surprise, a few of my friends invited me to join them in Maine, Boston, New York, and Virginia. I finally met up with Jill in Richmond after not seeing her for twelve years and found that our friendship is still strong and timeless. I thanked her for her generous support of me four decades earlier when we had walked by the James River and talked about our grandmothers, chickadees, and blue herons. In our last visit, over a light lunch of sandwiches and rose hip tea at the sumptuous Lewis Ginter Botanical Gardens, I reassured Jill that we will always have our sense of wonder to turn to.

"That's how we became friends—and why we're still friends." She beamed. I noticed her dimples and her easy smile. Her silver gray hair was softly pulled back by a lavender headband above her beaded hoop earrings. She spoke warmly of her retirement after forty years of social work, being able to nurture her family and friends, and potter with her backyard ferns and a mini waterfall.

After lunch, we strolled to her favorite spot in the gardens, a pathway of arched trellises covered with white and pink roses.

Notes

1 Dacher Keltner, *Awe: The New Science of Everyday Wonder and How It Can Transform Your Life* (New York: Penguin Books, 2023), 7.

2 Dacher Keltner, *Awe: The New Science of Everyday Wonder and How It Can Transform Your Life* (New York: Penguin Books, 2023), 39.

3 David Robson, "Awe: The little earthquake that could free your mind," *BBC*, January 6, 2022.

4 David Robson, "Awe: The little earthquake that could free your mind," *BBC*, January 6, 2022.

5 Anderson, C. L., Monroy, M., & Keltner, D. (2018). Awe in nature heals: Evidence from military veterans, at-risk youth, and college students. *Emotion, 18*(8), 1195–1202. https://doi.org/10.1037/emo0000442.

6   David Robson, "Awe: The little earthquake that could free your mind," *BBC*, January 6, 2022.

7   Stellar, J. E., Gordon, A., Anderson, C. L., Piff, P. K., McNeil, G. D., & Keltner, D. (2018). Awe and humility. *Journal of Personality and Social Psychology, 114*(2), 258–269. https://doi.org/10.1037/pspi0000109.

8   Stellar, J. E., John-Henderson, N., Anderson, C. L., Gordon, A. M., McNeil, G. D., & Keltner, D. (2015). Positive affect and markers of inflammation: Discrete positive emotions predict lower levels of inflammatory cytokines. *Emotion, 15*(2), 129–133. https://doi.org/10.1037/emo0000033.

9   Yaden, D. B., Kaufman, S. B., Hyde, E., Chirico, A., Gaggioli, A., Zhang, J. W., & Keltner, D. (2019). The development of the Awe Experience Scale (AWE-S): A multifactorial measure for a complex emotion. *The Journal of Positive Psychology, 14*(4), 474–488. https://doi.org/10.1080/17439760.2018.1484940.

10 Silvia, P. J., Fayn, K., & Beaty, R. E. (2015). Openness to experience and awe in response to nature and music: Personality and profound aesthetic experiences. *Psychology of Aesthetics, Creativity, and the Arts, 9*(4), 376–384. https://doi.org/10.1037/aca0000028.

PART II

STORIES OF HEALING THROUGH WONDER

Introducing Four Wondrous Profiles

In Part II, I share profiles of four people who deeply believe in the healing power of wonder for living with grief, trauma, and addiction. I am touched, thrilled, and enormously grateful for their honesty, courage, thoughtfulness, and generosity in telling their stories. I have personally found inspiration and hope from their recollections of how awe and wonder transformed their lives and sparked their faith in humanity.

For the Healing Through Wonder Project, I met the contributing storytellers through referrals from the following three organizations in the greater Boston area of Massachusetts (although two of the storytellers live in different states, Texas and Colorado):

- **The Sun Will Rise Foundation**
  The Sun Will Rise Foundation provides peer grief support for those who have experienced the death of someone they care about due to causes related to substance use.

- **SADOD (Support After a Death by Overdose)**
  SADOD is dedicated to increasing the effectiveness of peer grief support in Massachusetts for people affected by a death from substance use (not only from overdose but also from suicide, homicide, accident, and medical complications due to drug use).

- **The Health Story Collaborative**
  The mission of the Health Story Collaborative is to keep the patient voice alive in healthcare and to harness the healing power of stories. Annie Brewster, MD, the founder, is an assistant professor of medicine at Harvard Medical School, a practicing physician at Massachusetts General Hospital, and the author of *The Healing Power of Storytelling*.

The four storytellers come from different socioeconomic, ethnic, and racial backgrounds, but they've all benefited from awe and wonder in common ways, reflecting consistent findings in neuroscience research.

Even though each person has experienced a different source of awe and wonder, their stories demonstrate these common responses to awe:

- Shifting focus from our headspace (our self-referential, nagging thoughts) to what is outside of ourselves

- Self-transcendence and opening to a new perspective
- Being a part of something vast and much greater than ourselves (a small self)
- Feeling grounded and calmer in our bodies
- Time slowing down or standing still
- Seeing others in a new light and interest in helping others

In the following stories from **Robyn, Luke, Carol, and Ricky**, we can learn from their sense of wonder how powerful and profound our healing can be.

5

Robyn Houston-Bean

Living with Uncertainty Through Awe and Wonder

Awe and wonder experiences do not fix us or end our grief, but they help us move forward with hope.

Robyn Houston-Bean is the founder of the Sun Will Rise Foundation, a nonprofit organization dedicated to grief support for people who are bereaved due to substance-use-related causes. Her foundation was created after her twenty-year-old son, Nicholas Bean, died from an accidental polysubstance overdose in May 2015. Based in Braintree, Massachusetts, her nonprofit coordinates peer grief support groups, prevention programs, and community awareness events.

Around her outreach and advocacy, she owns an insurance agency with her father, David. She has been married to John since 1991, and they have two adult children, Jake and Olivia. Olivia volunteers as a graphic artist for the Sun Will Rise Foundation.

A warm, captivating speaker and storyteller, Robyn is energized by the mission of her dynamic organization, which began as a single support group for eight local parents in 2015 and has grown to 35 regular groups coordinated by thirty facilitators. In her outreach to parents, community members, and teens at schools and other venues, Robyn shares her family's story to let people know that substance use disorder can happen to any family or any one of us. "Our mission is to help erase the preconceived notions and stigma about people who have used substances."

After her son's death, Robyn acutely understands how stigma, shame, and isolation complicate grief, and how connection and community build resiliency for grieving people and those in recovery.

But it was a profound, life-changing experience of awe with a dragonfly that sparked her mission, long before she ever imagined how wondrous, wide, and generous the world could be.

Robyn's Story

Up to the day of her son's overdose, Robyn wholeheartedly believed his recovery from opioid use was progressing well.

> Nick was doing so well, and he was so proud of his new job as an emergency services technician. He told me almost every day how he loved his work, and loved being so helpful for others, saving lives. He had just gotten his certification, and he was so proud. He had a new mission in life. But maybe something triggered him. Maybe he saw too many horrible things during emergencies and rescues. Something must have upset him, but I will never know.

Robyn describes the night before the overdose when her daughter, Olivia, sensed Nick was unusually quiet and flat in his demeanor. She joined her daughter in the kitchen after Nick came home from work, trying to stifle her unease, affectionately checking in on him, gently putting her hands on the sides of his face and looking into his eyes.

> I asked if he was okay, and he replied, "I'm tired and going to bed. I have to be up for an early shift." But something in our last interaction still haunts me. Something was off, but I had no idea that something so horrible would happen that night.

The next morning, Robyn discovered his overdose.

> I was headed out to the gym for my usual workout. I saw Nick's car in the driveway, and this surprised me because he usually drove to work on the early shift. It seemed strange for him to leave the car there, and I started to worry. I called upstairs towards his room, "Hey Nick, are you up there?" But he didn't answer. I entered his room and found him motionless in his bed, cold and blue. I frantically tried to revive him with Narcan, but I could tell it was too late. I just screamed—an utterly gut-wrenching scream. Olivia called 911. The EMT and police came and took him to the hospital, but he was gone.

After Nick died, Robyn fell into despair and isolation. She spent weeks curled up on the couch, staring at the walls, unable to focus.

> When Nick died, I didn't know how to be me anymore. No one seemed to accept that the person I once was before Nick's death— that once unstoppable Robyn—no longer existed. I went from being a high-functioning go-getter to this shell of a person who

couldn't stop crying, who didn't want to do anything. I felt judged for having a son die from an overdose and being unable to save him, so I just wanted to be alone.

The Dragonfly

There was one single comforting routine that motivated Robyn to get off the couch and step out of her house. Her daily ritual was to drive to Nick's gravesite, only a couple of miles from her home. For several weeks before the headstone was placed, she sat alone on the soft, sun-soaked grass, finding private moments to pray, reminisce, and gently grieve.

But on the day she approached Nick's grave and saw the headstone permanently set in the ground, the reality of his death hit her much harder than what she was prepared to face, and suddenly and uncontrollably, she began to sob.

> I broke down and lay on the grass. I can even remember the smell of the ground, the earth. I felt that I couldn't go on any longer. I couldn't live my life without Nick. This wasn't how life was supposed to be. I didn't even want to get off the ground and stand up and walk. I was hysterical, curled up in a ball. But then, out of nowhere, a dragonfly appeared and hovered over me. He stayed with me. He came near my face and stared at me. We gazed at each other, and the whole world seemed to stop. My connection with the dragonfly lifted me out of my hysteria and pain. I sat up slowly, and it landed on my hand, and I just sat there as it looked towards

my face. I couldn't help but wonder if Nick was trying to connect with me. But whatever caused that dragonfly to stay with me, something miraculous had happened. I felt calmer and reassured that I would be okay.

Robyn describes how the dragonfly flew away for a minute but circled back to her and landed again on her hand. It spent another several minutes with her, softly resting on her hand, bringing her comfort with its delicate physical contact. Entranced, she sat with the dragonfly as the warm breezes passed across them together, inviting a sense of oneness and belonging.

It was so peaceful. I couldn't help but thank the dragonfly out loud. It had soothed me and brought me back to a world that I wanted to live in. To a greater reality where there was more to live for, a whole universe out there—and I was not alone. My life profoundly changed—and I'm forever grateful to that dragonfly!

This transformative experience radically opened Robyn to the realization that she could break out of her isolation and join a wider world where other grieving people were seeking connection. Her encounter with the dragonfly and her belief in her connection to her son's spirit sparked a sense of purpose.

My dragonfly moment *opened me up*. I had a huge revelation, and it all came down to this: I realized that my healing depended on being open to new experiences and new connections—reaching out. My child was not here anymore, but I could help someone else's child. I could help someone's family. And helping others could help me. This gave me a sense of purpose.

Robyn soon became Facebook friends with another grieving mother, who invited her to attend a group called Hand Delivered Hope, a nonprofit serving people living in active addiction on the street. Everyone volunteering had been impacted by a substance use disorder in some way and understood this disease. Robyn was touched by the warmth, compassion, and acceptance from the volunteers.

She recognized that the openness and humility she had felt during her dragonfly experience were essential qualities to being genuinely compassionate and accepting of others, particularly with those struggling with stigma and shame concerning substance use.

> Grieving is hard enough, but on top of that, a stigmatizing death can cause people to focus inward and avoid dealing with day-to-day life. It can cause grievers to be left alone in their grief by a community that doesn't know how to deal with loss. After my dragonfly experience, I could help others by showing up, and just being present, open, humble—what my moment of awe had taught me.

Robyn spotted a need for a support group in her local Braintree area and reached out to her mentor, Rhonda Lotti, a grief support facilitator of another group, who encouraged and guided her to start her own new group.

In honor of her son, Robyn named this group after what Nick had written on the cover of his notebook—two short sentences: "Please be happy. The sun will rise." Her organization, the Sun Will Rise, immediately welcomed eight people at the first meeting and quickly expanded over the next few months. With the help of her friend Rhonda, she networked easily with dozens of other groups throughout

New England, coordinating and promoting volunteer-driven new groups in nearby towns. Within months, she was coordinating groups for hundreds of families, as well as providing inspirational talks and fundraising events.

Sharing Awe and Wonder in Relationships and Groups

Ever since her dragonfly experience, Robyn has welcomed moments of wonder in her daily life. She enjoys "chasing wonder," as she describes marveling at the splendor of the natural world, as well as signs, synchronicities, dreams, and the amazing acts of courage she sees in people recovering from devastating losses.

> Once I opened myself to awe and wonder, I seem to find it all the time. I am not sure why, but I feel very lucky. Sometimes I don't realize right away just how amazing something is until I tell someone about it—and that person is wowed. Then *I* realize it, and we feel goose bumps together. Awe and wonder are contagious.

In her marriage, she intentionally invites moments of awe by encouraging her husband, John, to join her. She might wake him up at 2:00 a.m. to rush outside to watch the Northern Lights, or nudge him to take a look at her photo of a double rainbow. She admits she usually finds wonder before him, but "we are in it together when I show him."

A year after Nick died, Robyn and John visited the Muir Woods National Monument in California. They slowly walked hand in hand through the Redwood Forest, speechless and amazed.

It was humbling. If those giant old trees are still living here, we really don't know everything there is to know. We don't understand everything—but it's okay. I felt small in a good way. We felt a moment of peace accepting not having all the answers. Somewhere out there, Nick was there and maybe there was no end to him. This feeling of acceptance for not having all the answers was a healing step for us.

Robyn also enjoys experiencing awe on her own, as a soulful way to embrace her sense of belonging in the universe. "I love to listen to the wind while walking through a field or a forest. It's so simple, and yet so powerful."

She often travels to explore new adventures of "chasing wonder" in new ways. Determined to watch the 2024 solar eclipse in the path of totality, Robyn drove 600 miles alone to Ohio to find the best viewing spot.

It was worth the drive to get there, and I am so glad I went. It took my breath away. I got chills while the whole crowd gasped when it became dark. I felt a sense of oneness with complete strangers while we watched together. It was an intimate and vast experience all at once.

Robyn's wondrous experiences with nature have inspired her to share outdoor events with others who are grieving in her groups with the Sun Will Rise. She has facilitated ceremonies and rituals for grievers that elicit awe, reverence, and a sense of the sacred. On the coast of Massachusetts, one summer night under a full moon at the edge of the ocean, a group of thirteen women in unison called out the names of their deceased loved ones as they tossed wreaths into the waves.

> The healing is not just in the awe experience, it's in the sharing of it. Some of our grievers had lost loved ones during Covid and never had a chance to share their grief with anyone. It is so meaningful to have a whole group of grieving people calling out our person's name while standing in the moonlight by a magnificent ocean. We released our love for our people who have died into the vastness of the ocean and the night sky.

Robyn and her group facilitators regularly provide awe-inspiring activities, particularly at the beginning of a meeting to bring people together into a sacred sense of space. She witnesses how wondrous activities that take our breath away bring people into the present moment and out of their head space (negative inner self-talk). She knows group participants need moments of silence and quiet wonder to feel centered and grounded, and to connect with a sense of belonging.

She and her facilitators offer a candlelight ceremony at every support group meeting, including their meetings on Zoom. Participants say their loved one's name out loud at each meeting and pause for a moment of silence to gaze at the flame of the candle. Robyn appreciates using the phrase "awe and wonder moment" to invite new group members to share a sense of reverence that does not require a religious or spiritual connotation.

> People feel safer just calling these experiences "awe and wonder moments" as a universal, welcoming language. We encourage each other to share our stories of awe and wonder and reflect on how these experiences are helping us learn to live with grief. Some of the stories are similar to my experience with the Redwood Forest

where we felt small and saw the vastness around us. Other stories might be about dreams where loved ones who have passed have visited us. Or maybe we marvel at the way someone called us right when we were thinking about that person. These amazing experiences help us move forward even while we face uncertainty or things we cannot explain—we don't have to have all the answers.

Robyn organizes other community rituals through the Sun Will Rise, such as hanging thousands of small purple flags to memorialize deaths from overdose, gathering glow sticks together in a large vase in a solemn act of togetherness, reading poetry, releasing butterflies, candlelight vigils and walks, and sharing portraits of loved ones.

Awe brings people together. We give grievers an opportunity for openness and a greater sense of belonging. For example, we participated in a flag-planting event of 20,000 purple flags at Boston Common in 2024. Can you imagine how it felt to participate in that? Alongside thousands of other grievers, you planted your flag in honor of someone you loved who died from an opioid overdose. Your loved one's flag stands with a whole state of flags, revealing the huge impact of the opioid epidemic. The result was spectacular, absolutely amazing—Boston Common was covered in a sea of purple flags! Everyone could feel the amazement and power of that event.

Robyn believes people are hungry for group experiences of awe, but even further, she hopes that once a person has witnessed an awe-inspiring event in their community, they will continue to find personal awe experiences in their own lives. Even the simple act of telling someone about something that took our breath away can encourage that person to see wonder in a new light.

It's a gift to give people an opportunity to feel wonder with you, sharing something awe-inspiring together, or a story of awe. Once we have touched their sense of wonder, they are more likely to recognize wonder later on their own.

Awe and wonder experiences do not fix us or end our grief, but they help us move forward with hope.

How Wonder Helps Us Live with Uncertainty

Many of us during the pandemic felt overwhelmed by endless uncertainty and ambiguous losses, along with experiencing last-minute cancellations, being ghosted, let down, left hanging, and a host of other flaky behaviors. Unfortunately, much of that uncertainty and ambiguity continues today and may get worse. These tumultuous times call for ways to instill hope and meaning for moving forward and protecting and preserving our sense of wonder. Despite living in suspense and survival mode, we can turn to people like Robyn to inspire wonder, awe, and hope.

Not only does she know that moments of wonder are possible when bad news is always breaking, but she knows that wonder is *necessary* for surviving these uncertain times.

Fortunately, I've enjoyed a collaborative relationship with Robyn through our Healing Through Wonder Project. I've never met a person as genuinely open, accepting, and unabashedly wondrous.

She finds meaning and hope through her amazement and willingness to see through the many different lenses of the people she serves. Some people in her groups are hungry for spiritual or religious experiences of awe, and others are wowed by walks in the wilderness or by reading aloud a wondrous poem. No one has the last word on what is best for everyone, but anything that offers meaning and hope is welcome and shared. Fascinated by the wide, vast spectrum of healing experiences for survivors of grief, addiction, and trauma, her wellspring of wonder is the resilience of the human spirit.

> My healing comes from being open. My ability to help others comes from being open. I'm open to new experiences, open to learning and listening, open to living in uncertainty.

As open as she is, she is not overly optimistic or idealistic. Practical and realistic, she has managed an insurance agency for two decades, but her openness is not so profuse that her common sense and discretion disappear. (A well-known quote advises that we should not be too open-minded, or "not to be so open that your brains fall out," attributed to Walter Kotschnig, a professor at Holyoke College in 1940.)[1]

But we don't have to fall into nihilism or cynicism either.

Robyn shows us that we can be open, humble, grateful, and curious, but securely anchored by mature judgment and reasonable boundaries. Neuroscience research, using the 5-Factor Model of Personality (Big 5), consistently shows that openness to experience is a key personality component for finding awe and wonder.[2] Robyn displays this trait of openness as an exemplary role model for living with uncertainty as well as welcoming diversity and inclusion of people from all walks of life.

She goes with the flow better than most people I know, and certainly more successfully than I can. Her faith in her own sense of wonder has been stronger than mine, perhaps because she discovered this as a mature, middle-aged adult (unlike me at age twenty-four when a heron landed near me), or because she feels her son's spirit communicates with her through her moments of awe. She wholeheartedly believes in wonder, looks for it, finds it, delights in it—and it is contagious.

When I feel a humble, youthful sense of wonder in our interactions, I remember why I have so proactively chosen to live wondrously in these cynical, testy times. It's a breath of fresh air to share amazement with others—to pause and hold space for a bit of gratitude and beauty. She reassures me that wonder isn't just for kids or woo enthusiasts getting wowed by the latest conspiracy theory, drone or UAP sighting, plasmoid, haunted house, or new age prophecy.

Robyn reassures well-informed, even skeptical adults, with well-developed critical thinking skills and good, old-fashioned common sense, that we can *still* find magic and enchantment by *wondering* about inexplicable, miraculous, or mysterious experiences.

She encourages us to appreciate how breathtaking, mysterious moments help us live with uncertainty. The more we live with mystery and reverence for the mysterious, the better we can pivot around unexpected and inexplicable life events. Embracing mystery means we can explore, experiment, and play with ideas, feelings, and new experiences without needing to buy into belief systems hook, line, and sinker. If we are wondering about a dream, or a feather that lands at our door, or the afterlife, or just plain curious to learn more about these, our fascination doesn't mean we've become radicalized by a brand, belief, or manifesto, or that we've become fundamentalists or lost our minds. We just want to wonder.

And at the very least, wonder can be fun, restorative—and might add a dash of magic to snap us out of our funk. More deeply, wonder beckons us to find meaning, symbolism, new perspectives, and hope for moving forward in uncertain times. We search, quest, and explore as wonder seekers, or, as Robyn describes herself, as wonder chasers.

But what happens when we search for wonder online? For example, what if you wake up from a dream where a glowing angel appeared, and you're so intrigued that you jump on the internet in a feverish quest to learn about angels in dreams? Imagine how your online search for, say, "angels in dreams," winds up sending you through hundreds of links to dream interpretation websites and spiritual message websites, getting you hooked into whatever AI and algorithms tell you to wonder about.

Your digital quest for angel lore can be a double-edged sword: Yes, your search instantly takes you far on your wonder journey—but wait, you end up viewing a video where God tells you to prepare for the apocalypse, or channeled ETs implore you to shift to a higher vibration of fifth-dimensional consciousness.

Our wonder-infused online searches *do the wondering for us*. But those algorithms might take us *way* off course from that exquisite, personal experience of wonder we had with our angel. We need to be careful not to fall through rabbit holes and land in oversaturated virtual realities that distract, diminish, or snuff out our spark of wonder.

Algorithms and AI can take away the magic from our wondrous moments, or perhaps their power.

This is why I tend to stay offline when I wonder about my dreams, at least at first, when I wake up and sit with my coffee. I would rather just savor a glorious dream and greet the day with an open heart. And later, why not explore my dream through a long talk with a friend, a song, or traveling to a whole new river or mountaintop?

I turn to Robyn again for inspiration. Many of us need people like her to help preserve and cultivate our sense of wonder—to wonder out loud, to learn, to explore, to walk, to share dreams and stories. Our common bond between my heron encounter and her dragonfly moment has built a sacred bond. Our awe experiences are not only self-transcending experiences, but when shared, they transcend our relationship.

Robyn doesn't hold back the joy of her wonderful encounters, no matter how simple or small. As in the old saying "Come on in, the water's fine," she asks us to join in her wonder.

She knows I don't need to justify why I had a glorious angel dream or a blue heron encounter that made me wonder if my grandmother Viv was speaking to me. Or that I can feel the whiskers and soft purring of my beloved (deceased) cat Ivan appearing in a dream to love me to pieces. Robyn agrees that no one has the last word on whether these are real experiences or not. Likewise, she can find guidance from her deceased son through a dragonfly, a rainbow, or a visit in a dream, and I am honored that she wants me to share her hope.

And hope shared is hope strengthened.

Why not find meaning, beauty, or guidance through sharing these encounters or epiphanies?

We can put inexplicable or mysterious experiences or possibilities "on the shelf" for those (not-quite) plausible things, as my friend

Jill once told me. We can allow divergent thinking, or agnostic, or pluralistic, or "both-and" ways of thinking rather than "either-or" frameworks. We can hold space for ambiguous, contradictory, or incongruent thoughts somewhere in our minds alongside our more solid beliefs if we make time for reflection, contemplation, or even creating art (brilliant fictional characters and songs come from inexplicable things). Open and imaginative minds are willing to hold the tension of divergent, perplexing, and unsettled thoughts and explore them, often through empathy, curiosity—and wonder—*what is it like to think that way? Or feel that way?*

Robyn beckons me to spend less time explaining, justifying, or rationalizing these mysterious encounters and to bask in the meaning, hope, and renewal these moments give me.

But the most heartening gift of Robyn's openness for me, and other trauma and grief survivors, is her willingness to live with the uncertainty of unresolved and multiple losses. Her embrace of mystery and bringing experiences of awe and wonder to her groups reassures grievers that moments of peace and serenity are possible, especially through regular rituals at her support groups. This intentional inclusion of awe-enhancing activities is supported by a study published by the American Psychological Association in 2020, "Awe-ful Uncertainty: Easing Discomfort During Waiting Periods." The findings demonstrated that people coping with uncertain life situations benefited from reduced anxiety by engaging in experiences of awe.[3]

Awe and wonder help us live with uncertainty and unresolved grief and trauma. Instead of racing ahead trying to "get over it," we can allow ourselves to heal at our own pace and remain open to our own unique experiences of healing. By allowing for uncertainty and mystery, we can appreciate the way our acceptance of loss unfolds in its own time. Our sense of mystery and wonder shows us how uncertain, unpredictable, and surprising events often bring us meaning and purpose. Some people call this meaningful unfolding of time "divine timing," others call this natural, unforced timing "right timing," or sacred timing.

Robyn's embrace of mystery, wonder, and uncertainty in her healing journey reflects the findings of grief researchers over the past fifteen years that grieving is a personal, individual journey, often unpredictable, unique, and different for each of us. Researchers have moved beyond earlier theories of healing, especially the modality of the five stages of grief by Elizabeth Kubler Ross, and now advise us not to try to fit our experiences into stages or timetables.[4] Indeed, comparing ourselves to others in terms of whether we are going through our grief the "right way" can complicate our grieving. Although the process is messy, murky, and erratic at times, it helps to be open and compassionate with ourselves and embrace our own path, as uncertain as the journey may be. Robyn encourages us to allow this open, gentle approach, accepting ourselves rather than fixing ourselves.

Prominent researchers such as Kenneth Doka (*Grief Is a Journey*) and Pauline Boss (*The Myth of Closure*) reassure us that surviving grief does not require passing through all the stages of grief or "working" through our stages in any particular order. Instead, we can learn to live with grief by finding meaning and hope in our own individual journey, not expecting to find closure or "get over it" according to someone else's timetable. Furthermore, researchers recommend resilience-building activities through awe, creativity, helping others, community, and other purposeful expressions as ways to instill meaning and hope.

As Robyn inspires us, grief moves through us by keeping open to new experiences and wider perspectives. It all comes down to openness. When her group of thirteen women stood by the ocean in the moonlight, calling out the names of their loved ones, out across the ocean waves, out into the wide starry night, they opened themselves to a sacred moment. Their grief, love, and reverence for life all came together as they sent their wreaths out into the sea.

They had faith, somehow, that this mysterious, beautiful vastness would hold dear something precious given from their hands and hearts.

This reminds me of the time, after the end of my marriage, on the coast of Maine, I hiked to the rocky, windy headlands jutting out between frothy water and sky. In my own private ritual, I put my wedding ring in a tiny wooden box with a prayer and threw it far into the froth. Who knows, I sighed. Someone might be happy to find it someday.

Healing grief is an act of faith, like sending out a message in a bottle or releasing a precious thing into the ocean. We are not sure if it will end up in good hands somewhere far away, but we send it anyway—just in case it does.

We can let the vast, mysterious universe take what we release, even our grief, in case it ends up in good hands out there somewhere.

Robyn's Wonder Wisdom in a Nutshell

What causes people to lose their sense of wonder?

People lose their sense of wonder when they lose hope.
They don't try new activities.
They don't risk anything.
They don't look forward to anything.

What helps trauma survivors heal through wonder?

Appreciate the little wonders, the little surprises, see the beauty around you.
Notice the concrete, physical things, the things you can touch (to ground yourself).
Take a walk.
Listen to the wind.
Be willing to share your story of a wondrous thing (it might inspire someone else).

Why are wonder and awe important for living in these times?

We can forget what awe and wonder feel like, and lose touch with this part of ourselves.
We forget to live in our bodies and live too much in our heads.
We need a sense of wonder to keep us connected to the world outside of ourselves.
If we don't have wonder, we think we are all alone, and our pain is ours alone—and that makes us lonely.

What are your favorite wondrous quotes?

"Please be happy. The sun will rise."
—Nick Bean, Robyn's son

"Tell me, what is it you plan to do
with your one wild and precious life?"
—Mary Oliver

"In every walk with nature, one receives far more than he seeks."
—John Muir

What wondrous book do you recommend?

Tuesdays with Morrie by Mitch Albom

What wondrous movie or video do you recommend?

Interstellar

What wondrous music or song do you recommend?

"Fix You" by Coldplay, particularly the version of Chris Martin singing with Michael J. Fox at the Glastonbury Music Festival (available on YouTube)

Who is an awe-inspiring celebrity/famous person, a role model of openly wondrous and joyous behavior?

Brandon Stanton, the creator of *Humans of New York*

Notes

1. Jonathan Becher, "Keep an open mind," *Forbes*, October 6, 2014.

2. Dong, R., & Ni, S. G. (2020). Openness to experience, extraversion, and subjective well-being among Chinese college students: The mediating role of dispositional awe. *Psychological Reports, 123*(3), 903–928. https://doi.org/10.1177/0033294119826884.

3. Rankin, K., Andrews, S. E., & Sweeny, K. (2019). Awe-full uncertainty: Easing discomfort during waiting periods. *The Journal of Positive Psychology, 15*(3), 338–347. https://doi.org/10.1080/17439760.2019.1615106.

4. Patrick White, "Why psychologists want us to stop talking about the 'five stages' of grief," *ABC Lifestyle,* August 14, 2024.

6

Luke Schmaltz
Finding Wonder in Everyday Conversations

I find awe in people and reflect it back to them.
Awe helps you see beauty in others and in the world around you.

Luke Schmaltz is a songwriter, singer, writer, and an advocate for trauma survivors and others in recovery. He lives in Denver, Colorado, and has been married for twelve years. He grew up in Albuquerque, New Mexico, raised in a Catholic family while attending a Catholic school from first through eighth grade. He was especially close to his brother during these years.

Luke's Story

My brother is eleven months older than me. And my sister is three years older than me. My brother and I were the same size up until the ages of twelve and thirteen. We did everything together and fought, somewhat playfully, somewhat fiercely, every day. When he growth-spurted into a monster at thirteen, he didn't let his physical advantages go to his already brilliant head. We remained close with an unshakable bond, which endures to this day. My father was a veterinarian, and my mother was an English teacher, a realtor, a tech marketer, and an entrepreneur. They instilled in me a distinct moral code, aligned with doing the right thing, even when it seemed too hard. Despite the trauma, I was blessed with a loving family.

Unfortunately, all three of us were deeply traumatized by our grandpa when we were very little, which somehow drew us closer together. I was the youngest, and my siblings truly looked out for me. The trauma made us all hypervigilant, and nearly fearless when dealing with predatory people. At thirteen, my brother turned into my protector because I was still a shrimp through high school. He was my best friend.

Sadly, in addition to being abused by his grandfather, he suffered more severe abuse at his school. Luke describes being "groomed" for sexual abuse by a priest in the third grade, and then being molested and raped at eleven years old.

> He started grooming me for sexual abuse in the third grade. At eleven, the rape did some really significant physical, emotional, and psychological damage. But he also terrorized me repeatedly until the age of fourteen through threatening phone calls, saying that if I ever told anybody he was going to kill me.

During those years, Luke relied on his brother for companionship and emotional support, although he kept the abuse hidden from him and others in the family.

A few years later, when he was eighteen, his brother was in a brutal car accident, suffering severe injuries including a broken pelvis and spine. He ended up in the ICU, in a coma, and was not expected to live.

Luke sat by his bedside in the hospital, believing his brother would die, and trying to prepare himself for Last Rites (a Catholic ritual of prayers and sacraments for people who are dying), scheduled for later that day. "My brother, my best friend, was dying in front of me."

Unfortunately, at this time, Luke's perpetrator, the priest (who had been demoted), was now a chaplain for the hospital. "The priest had changed his name by then because he had gotten in trouble for doing to other kids what he had done to me."

This chaplain walked into the room to perform Last Rites for Luke's brother. They instantly recognized each other. Shocked and horrified, Luke stood up, feeling a surge of emotions of fierce protection for his brother as well as raw rage at seeing his perpetrator. He did not want this man to have access to his brother, and his instincts kicked into full gear.

> Something erupted in me. I yelled with the force of emotion and rage that probably shook the rafters of the place. I said, "You get the F out of here! We don't want your Last Rites! Leave now!" He kind of turned white and backed out of the room. Then the door closed. And then—I heard my brother's voice say, "Hey, what the hell was that?" So somehow my screaming at the priest pulled my brother out of his coma!

Amazingly, Luke's rage and act of protection sparked his brother to come out of his coma. The astounding alignment of Luke, his brother, and his perpetrator all in the same room at once somehow caused the intense energy of that encounter to rouse his brother from his deep, near-deathly sleep.

Dumbfounded, awestruck, Luke welcomed his brother back to consciousness. He didn't tell his brother what had woken him up from his coma, but he reassured him, "It was nothing, don't worry." Excited and eager to communicate, Luke interacted with his brother and helped him adjust to being awake and oriented.

His brother began his recovery after this lifesaving event. He had multiple surgeries over two years but returned to his normal activities, including his job and his pastimes: hunting and other outdoor sports.

Luke believes that his brother's sudden emergence from a coma is a miraculous, inexplicable gift. "I don't want to diminish the power of this by trying to explain it because it was an exceptional situation. I accept it for what it is." He does not feel the need to analyze how the strong emotions and yelling in the room woke up his brother, or how incredible it was that the same man who had abused him as a child showed up in the same hospital room at that particular time. "All I know is that it happened on an atomic level or a cellular level, and it was an instance of awe and wonder."

The breathtaking moment of hearing his brother speak as he apparently lay dying in a coma profoundly transformed Luke. He witnessed the return of his brother's voice immediately after he had used his own voice to confront the priest.

> It was a catalyst for me. That eruption of emotion somehow shook my brother out of that coma—but it also demonstrated to me how it's really important to stand up for myself and others, and to vocalize my observations and emotions.

The Wonder of Voice

This awe experience deeply inspired Luke to use the power and agency of his voice in creative and purposeful ways throughout his life. Ever since, he has been a songwriter, singer, writer, and advocate. "I started a punk rock band called King Rat in 1994 and it just turned thirty. So I've been in this band longer than I haven't." He tours Colorado and the Mountain West and Midwest regions with his band and also plays as a solo acoustic performer.

He describes being in awe of people every day, always fascinated by the way people communicate with words. He describes how his mind is open to awe because he is in a creative "songwriting mode" that allows him to take note of the fascinating world around him.

> I am always in songwriting mode in one way, shape, or form. It's like the valve is always open so I am always open. I look for little nuggets of conversation. I listen—and then tell them, wow, what they said is awesome. I will pull out my pen and scribble it down to remember it. I look for awe in the way people talk—I find awe in language. A lot of my songs come from observing instances of awe and wonder in others. I might pick up on this in dream states or through conversations. I find awe in people and reflect it back to them.

Luke also reflects back the awe he sees in people through his writing. He is a fiction author and a freelance writer for many newsletters and blogs for a wide variety of outlets. Particularly after 2016, when he became a member of SNAP (Survivors Network of those Abused by

Priests), he has directed his writing towards advocacy and outreach. He is an avid supporter of SNAP and regularly attends support groups in the Denver area.

On a spiritual and metaphorical level, he has been carrying out his mission of serving as a voice, speaking out on behalf of the rights, protections, and independence of others—as he did when he confronted the priest and protected his brother. It is no surprise that in 2022 he became the editor of a newsletter called *VOICES*, a monthly newsletter for SADOD (Support After a Death from Overdose). He profiles bereaved people as well as those in recovery, peer grief volunteers, and direct service providers.

Luke's ability and passion for finding awe in people and drawing out their recovery stories is a gift for those he profiles and interviews. Through his vibrant sense of wonder, he beckons his interviewees to openly explore aspects of themselves that they have rarely considered, let alone shared with others. He invites people to wonder out loud by telling their life stories. His fascination and curiosity shine a light on other people's sense of wonder and openness.

Luke believes that his psychotherapy since the age of forty-six (he's now fifty-three) and his involvement with SNAP and their support groups have been crucial in his recovery.

> It was a necessity for me. I was going to sabotage my marriage if I didn't get help. Professional therapy and peer group support is essential. I needed to examine the trauma and abuse from a 360-degree angle outside of my head instead of in my own thoughts that were arguing with each other. And being with people who had experienced the same exact trauma was a huge benefit. I have met wonderful people in SNAP.

Luke has read *The Body Keeps the Score* by Bessel van der Kolk and shared this book and his interest in trauma recovery with his brother. His brother recently began EMDR therapy. They support each other in their healing, and Luke finds his brother's support and enthusiasm in his recovery deeply empowering and heartening.

Luke has often found awe through his amazement in the courageous and generous acts of others. One of these heroes in his life is his wife, Christal. He is in awe of her courage and willingness to stand up for him. "I will always be awestruck by what she has done to help me. It's profound. She has shown me that I deserve love."

Another awe moment in Luke's life occurred when two enormous life-changing events happened on the same day in May 2022. After waiting for several years, Luke was finally notified that the Archdiocese of Santa Fe had reached a settlement of $121.5 million to resolve a bankruptcy case over many sexual abuse claims—including Luke's claim concerning his childhood abuse by the priest. Simultaneously, Luke received news of a job offer to be the editor of *VOICES* for SADOD. The astounding concurrence of these events signaled a powerful green light for Luke that it was worth fighting for justice and using his voice to build community and advocate for others. "Both of these had been a long shot, but they came through on the same day!" Even though Luke jokes that he was a "lucky dog" on that day and that his ship had finally come in, he marvels at the synchronicity and beautiful timing that these events happened simultaneously. He took these to be a blessing, giving him reassurance, stamina, and hope to continue his life mission to stand up for the rights of trauma survivors and people in recovery through his writing, songs, and storytelling.

Reflecting more on the healing power of awe and wonder for trauma survivors in general, he adds:

> Awe changes your focus from ugliness to beauty. Trauma survivors tend to look for the ugly to happen and we have our guard up. We expect someone will screw you over, or the other shoe will drop, or someone you trust will betray you. If you spend too much time in that energy, you will find ugliness and just keep feeding the trauma. But if you focus on awe and beauty, then you are going to encounter more of that. Awe helps you see beauty—in others, and in the world around you.

He wonders how awe opens trauma survivors to find more opportunities for healing. He believes sharing stories about awe experiences can show other survivors how to find it. Being willing and open is key. He is convinced we can simply forget our awe moments, especially if we never talk about them.

> You might have more wonder than you think if you can just be aware of the small things in the world around you. If you are turned off to the possibility that something exceptional is ever going to happen, then you won't be open to receiving it when it does.

Luke considers the uncanny synchronistic moments that have occurred recently in his life. He notices that these astounding events happen more frequently because he is more open-minded and receptive to these moments. He recalls an amazing connection the previous week while interviewing a community leader for the *VOICES* newsletter for SADOD. He shares a mutual moment of awe.

I was interviewing the executive director of a grief support organization for children and families in the Boston area. He told me about a silver belt buckle his father had given him. He described his father as a "cowboy from Albuquerque." I was amazed because *I* have a father who *also* gave me a belt buckle and who is *also* a "cowboy from Albuquerque." These special belt buckles have *such* deep meaning for us. It is a lot more than a coincidence how our connections line up! How does this happen? I felt real awe—I think we both felt awe.

Luke joyously appreciates the benefits of sharing stories of wonder, synchronicities and signs, spiritual experiences, and moments of sheer awe. He believes the more people share their stories and speak openly about their awe and wonder, the more sensitized and aware we become of the wider world as well as our interactions with *each other*. Luke reminds us that awe does not have to come from a powerful experience in nature, a supernatural event, or an exotic trip. We can spot wonder in a fleeting, brief conversation and instantly find a meaningful connection. Or we can make meaning out of a random conversation by finding a message in the timing of the delivery of that message. As in the belt buckle story of the two fathers who were "cowboys from Albuquerque," we can enjoy these little discoveries in our casual interactions.

These occurrences happen naturally in our most relaxed, spontaneous conversations. Many of us have witnessed these marvelous little surprises that pop up in the course of chatting. "Oh wow, what you just said is amazing—I was thinking that very same thing today."

Luke believes that our interest in others naturally draws awe into the interaction, as long as we pause and listen.

We need to hold space with one another for the wonder to emerge.

Just by giving people the gift of your time, your meaningful way of saying, "Hello, how are you?" and by listening wholeheartedly without interrupting them, you are allowing awe and wonder to emerge. You can see a change in their facial expression, their body language, and their general sense of ease.

Luke finds wonder in conversations like these—and does not hold back from showing his amazement. His wonderment is warm, welcoming, and puts people at ease. He draws out a spontaneous, youthful, and genuine sense of wonder in the people with whom he engages. He lifts people out of their headspace into the present moment. Whether he is sitting at a SNAP support group with fellow trauma survivors, interviewing a community leader for a newsletter, or performing his songs, Luke brings the wide world of wonder into his interactions.

The Art of Finding Wonder in People

Too often, we forget about these amazing yet fleeting conversational moments that Luke describes. We are spellbound for a couple of minutes, but the excitement fades. We lose the magic.

Then we get back on our phones.

Unlike Luke, unfortunately, I'm the first to admit that I've grown wary of casual in-person human interaction. I've adopted more calculated and detached behaviors since 2020—survival mode, but it's lonely. Compared to pre-pandemic times when I shared my wondrous, curious side with people more easily and fluidly, I'm tired and guarded, fearing a palpable testiness in almost everyone (particularly after the 2024 US election). Like most people these days, I look at my phone and avoid contact, not so much because I love what's onscreen, but because getting into a conversation could mean getting into trouble.

Changes in social behavior echo studies showing that Americans are less likely to spontaneously chat or even just hang out together. In an alarming article in the *Atlantic* (February 2024), Derek Thompson reports that the number of hours Americans spend in face-to-face interactions has dropped 30 percent in twenty years (between 2003 and 2022).[1] For teenagers, the decline is 45 percent.

Anxiety and fear of social judgment are tongue-tying us. Generation Z and younger people are far less inclined to chat or wonder openly with others in person. Petrified of saying the wrong thing, they err on the side of saying nothing because in-person conversation is harshly scrutinized. It might be easier to post your opinions on TikTok or Instagram than to directly discuss your point of view with a sibling or a friend. Jonathan Haidt, in his bestseller, *The Anxious Generation: How the Great Rewiring of Childhood Is Causing an Epidemic of Mental Illness,* exposes how American children have too much screen time and not enough autonomy. He observes that teens are overprotected in the real world but underprotected online.[2] This creates a fear of interacting in person, especially while in public, working, exploring, traveling, learning, and being out in the world having adventures and new experiences—these unpredictable, inexplicable, fascinating experiences that give us awe and wonder!

Overall, as a society, we've become risk-averse to thinking out loud, let alone wondering out loud. But we miss each other's wonder and joy by being judgmental, testy, and rushed.

I marvel at Luke's willingness to be wondrous about people. I'm inspired by his ability to spot synchronicities, signs, and meanings in natural conversations through his curiosity and awe in his everyday interactions. By openly exploring people through the interviews and profiles he writes for the *VOICES* newsletter, as well as songwriting and fiction writing, his wonder percolates through his inquisitive, creative personality—and it's contagious.

Luke's awe of the people he encounters is refreshing and reassuring for those of us who have been losing faith in humanity. Even though Luke is cynical about politics, government, and authority figures in general, he is fascinated by everyday encounters with his colleagues, neighbors, friends, and family members. He has so many aha moments with people that he wonders if he could benefit from keeping a journal or log of his ever-increasing synchronistic and serendipitous events with people around him. "It's good to keep track of moments that take your breath away."

When he considers how sharing stories of awe and wonder experiences could help trauma survivors in support groups (such as groups for sexual abuse survivors at SNAP), he believes it might be helpful at a later stage of recovery if the group members feel safe enough to share these. He explains that earlier in their recovery, survivors are just trying to grapple with what happened to them and cannot wrap their minds around more than building a language of trust between survivors.

> It's a very specific kind of trauma to be the survivor of sexual abuse by a priest, and survivors need to find each other first and build that trust. Newcomers to the groups can barely talk about why they're there. They're hanging on for dear life—just trying to sit in the group and listen.

Luke deeply believes that healing through wonder and awe is most effective when we share our experiences to break through isolation. Trauma survivors can lose their sense of wonder if they are too isolated and withdrawn from meaningful social interactions. And yet he recognizes that sharing a moment of awe with someone in a conversation (such as at a support group) can restore our sense of wonder. In short, we need human interaction to draw out the wonder of each other—and to preserve our sense of wonder.

> People lose their sense of awe and wonder due to isolation. The negative thought patterns that build upon themselves into formidable barriers can convince a traumatized person that all pursuits of happiness and joy are useless, and every effort will end in disappointment. Connection is key, whether it is with another human, or an animal, or a breathtaking landscape.

Luke recognizes that wonder in action through connection is crucial to a trauma survivor's hope for healing, as well as for keeping faith in humanity. After six years of psychotherapy, being part of SNAP support groups, and sharing his healing with his brother, Luke is confident that our experiences of awe are gifts to others when shared through conversation and stories.

Luke's Wonder Wisdom in a Nutshell

What causes people to lose their sense of wonder?

People lose their sense of wonder due to isolation, guardedness, and distraction.

Isolation, avoiding conversation and interactions

Being too caught up in your headspace

Not noticing a sense of connection in nature and animals

Lack of creative expression through the arts or through serving others

What helps trauma survivors heal through wonder?

Connection is key, whether it is with another human, or an animal, or a breathtaking landscape.

Shifting your focus to something or someone outside of yourself

Being out of your headspace

Finding wonder in everyday conversations

Noticing the amazing things people do

Being grateful for the amazing things people say and do

Why are wonder and awe important for living in these times?

Wonder restores our faith in humanity and makes us more compassionate.

Wonder keeps us from relying too much on technology.

Wonder keeps us from being unfocused and distracted.
Wonder gives us hope.

What are your favorite wondrous quotes?

"O wad some power the giftie gie us to see oursels as others see us!"
—Robert Burns, "To A Louse, On Seeing One on a Lady's Bonnet at Church"
"It's never too late to have a happy childhood."
—Tom Robbins

What wondrous book(s) do you recommend?

The Giving Tree by Shel Silverstein
Where the Sidewalk Ends by Shel Silverstein
Stranger in a Strange Land by Robert Heinlein

What wondrous movie or video do you recommend?

Blade Runner
Star Wars: A New Hope
Star Wars: The Empire Strikes Back
Shawshank Redemption

What wondrous music or song do you recommend?

Any album by the Pixies, but preferably *Doolittle, Trompe le Monde, Come on, Pilgrim*

Who are some awe-inspiring celebrities/famous people who are role models of openly wondrous and joyous behaviors?

Robin Williams

Carol Burnett

Steve Martin

Notes

1. Derek Thompson, "Why Americans suddenly stopped hanging out," *Atlantic*, February 14, 2024.
2. Michaeleen Doucleff, "How to give kids autonomy? 'Anxious Generation' author says a license to roam helps," *NPR*, April 14, 2024.

7

Carol Bowers
Healing Through Sharing Awe and Wonder

Wonder is everywhere if you are willing to see it.

Carol has a natural way of putting people at ease. Warm, open, and honest, she invites conversation with her genuine kindness and interest in others. She often volunteers with local recovery and peer grief support organizations in the greater Boston area. She is the proud mother of a daughter and son, with five grandchildren and two great-grandchildren. Her husband, Jeff, died in 2022 after a strong, loving partnership of thirty-one years. She is immensely proud of her son, Timmy, who has been in recovery for many years. She believes he has broken the cycle of addiction in her family.

She works with groups to help create safe places for people to grieve and openly heal by sharing their stories. "It's okay to be completely vulnerable with someone—it's an honor. When we share this vulnerability, it doesn't have the weight on you."

"I identify with most people. I say 'me too' a lot. When I was thirteen, my friends called me Dear Abby. People have always felt safe opening up to me. I was born with a lot of empathy, and I am thankful I have this gift." She believes her own best qualities come from her mother, Rita, who died at the age of ninety-six in 2013. "My empathy, my determination, my loyalty come from her. I am also grateful for learning survival skills from her that have made me resilient."

Carol's Story

Carol is the youngest of six children, raised by her single mother in a working-class neighborhood in Lawrence, Massachusetts, in the 1960s and early 1970s.

> I had a lot of responsibility, helping my mother. It was a survival world. I remember how hard my mother worked to raise us. On Easter, for example, I remember her ironing our dresses with starch, for hours and hours. She was always there for us—she loved us—but she was really exhausted by the time I turned thirteen. She was working full time at a textile mill at that time.

Carol didn't have any specific memories about moments of wonder as a child, but she recalls spending time with her doll named Joey.

> I made my own fun, playing with my doll in a little nook off of a hallway. It was my own little spot where I lived in my own world. There was a window in that nook, and I imagined all kinds of faraway places looking out of that window.

Later, with her lively imagination and hungry for magical moments and fantasy, she fell in love with art at school. "My teachers encouraged me in ceramics and crafts, and I loved to create things. All children have wonder, as I did, but little by little, my life chipped away at my sense of wonder because I had to survive and take care of myself. The older I got, the less freedom I had."

Carol's friends in high school were already using heroin when she was fourteen. She was able to fend off the peer pressure to try it at parties for a year.

> When I was fifteen, I started using heroin. I remember the first day I used, how I was upset at my boyfriend and wanted something to feel better. I would leave school at lunchtime and walk about five minutes away to buy the drugs. Then I would come back to school and use in the bathrooms. Already many of my friends were using—and it was so easy to do. I would say that I used drugs in the beginning, but later those drugs used *me*.

Carol describes how using heroin gave her a sense of awe and wonder.

> I got instant awe and wonder using drugs. I felt like I had been robbed from having wonder in my younger life because I was in survival mode as a teen. Using drugs was magical—it gave me a sense of freedom like I could be whoever I wanted to be. . . . But heroin swallowed up my life. I used right up to the age of thirty-nine. In 1991, I went to detox weighing only seventy pounds. Then, I went to a treatment center in East Boston.

Carol was adamant that no matter how difficult her addiction became, her mother never abandoned her and always believed in her. "My mother never walked away from me. She had unconditional love. No matter how bad off I was, she was always right there for me."

About four months after living at the treatment center, Carol was given an eight-hour, one-day pass to spend the day with a sponsor. "But fifteen minutes into the day, my plan went astray. I turned around (instead of going to my sponsor) and headed to Lawrence to go to my using place. Being clean just didn't feel real to me. It seemed inevitable that I would eventually use again."

By this point, a relapse was likely to happen on this day. She hitched a ride on a large truck. The friendly driver had the radio on, and she was starting to feel excited about using again in Lawrence, already enjoying the freedom of cruising down the road, sitting in the front seat.

Out of the blue, taking her by surprise, a song came on the radio that Carol had not heard for many months. Wilson Phillips was blasting out their song "Hold On."

Break free, break from the chains.
Hold on for one more day.

Suddenly, these words spoke to Carol, and her whole world changed with a powerful burst of awe. How amazing that these words could express such a perfect message at the perfect time—divine timing! The message was profound—*break free from the chains. Hold on for one more day.*

Deep in her bones, she felt a chill of truth. Yes, she could hold on for just one more day—and not use any drug today. She did not have to use again. It was not an automatic, inevitable fact that she would relapse today. She had the choice to break out of those chains.

"God was speaking to me—it saved my life," she marvels out loud. "It was a miracle."

She suspects that if it had been any other song, even other songs she liked, none of them would have had the same impact. "No other song could have done that to me! . . . That song broke me. It broke through to me. It broke me out of my chains."

Carol described being so moved by the song that she couldn't stop sobbing in front of the truck driver. She asked him to please let her out of the truck, and he pulled over for her to exit. Carol was so stunned and so emotional from the song that she sat for an hour near a tree to process her powerful healing. "I've never cried like that. This was a truth so deep."

Soon she phoned her daughter from a pay phone, and fortunately, was able to spend the night with her because the treatment center was not an option at that point. "I had nowhere else to go."

But ever since that day in 1991, Carol has not used. "When I woke up at my daughter's the next day, I didn't want to use. This was a miraculous revelation for me. I had never thought about using and not used. The blessing of that song had carried me through."

Jeff

Soon she moved to the South Shore area of Massachusetts. "My real recovery started at that time." She reconnected with a peer in recovery named Jeff, whom she had first met at the treatment center in East Boston. He became her partner for thirty-one years, and they were married for fourteen years of that time. She and Jeff began their relationship with a solid commitment to their recovery. "We built a life through our recovery and learned what a healthy relationship was like."

Both Carol and Jeff served as enthusiastic volunteers for recovery and substance use prevention initiatives in their local community. Carol reached out to people in recovery as a speaker, including high school students, and Jeff worked with homeless veterans in recovery and at a local VA hospital. Jeff was a popular inspirational speaker and advocate.

> My husband had a gift with his message. He didn't like being in the limelight, but he was asked to speak at many international conventions for veterans and other groups. He was an incredible speaker because he could touch people from all backgrounds. He helped thousands of people.

In 2020, after thirty-one years of not using substances, Jeff unfortunately became seriously ill with Covid-19. Carol explains that the inflammation affected the arthritis in his spine. "The Covid settled in his spine. He couldn't lie down or sit up for weeks and was in terrible agony." Jeff was prescribed painkillers and became addicted. "Somewhere he ended up crossing the line and began using street drugs." But he was able to hide his use from Carol. She was amazed when he admitted to her three months later that he had relapsed in such a dire, life-threatening way. He announced he would stop using, and for the next nine months, he struggled. But every day she could see he was suffering. "It was hard for him to even want to live."

On March 31, 2022, Jeff overdosed on fentanyl.

The death of her husband was not only unbearable, it was *unsharable* for Carol. "It was the stigma that got in the way—I just didn't feel I could trust anyone to talk about his overdose." Carol was not only devastated by grief, but she ruminated about the stigma of this overdose because her husband had been so well-known and respected as an advocate for recovery throughout the Boston area.

"I'm very protective of the people I love. I was hesitant to talk about what happened. Jeff had given so much to so many others, not just me." Carol's grief was painfully lonely. As vulnerable as she might have been to a relapse, she was highly determined to stick to her recovery. Fortunately, she recognized her own vulnerabilities and began to consider going to a grief support group—but still, the stigma and shame gripped her in isolation. She could tell she was in trouble. "I was having the toughest time. I was committed to my recovery, but I wasn't getting what I needed—and I wasn't sure what it was that I needed."

Somehow, Carol's inner voice led her to believe that she needed a community of support. She and Jeff had seen the power of that support in recovery from addiction, but what about a community for the particular pain of grief due to overdose?

Amazingly, soon after Jeff's death, she received a card in the mail to join a group from the Sun Will Rise Foundation. Carol was alarmed at first to receive this invitation to a support group because she feared the group members might not understand the stigma around overdose or substance use. She spoke with the founder of the group and was reassured that the group members were all dealing with the same stigma and isolation around their grief. She bravely decided to give the group a chance and was relieved by the acceptance and understanding of the participants. For a year, this was a helpful community for Carol, but eventually, she felt herself falling into a dark, stagnant place in her grief and became aware that she needed individual counseling. "It was time to go deeper and talk to someone really closely. Something in me needed a much closer, more understanding connection." The Sun Will Rise Foundation connected her to a peer grief ally named Leslie.

Holding On

Carol experienced a profound moment of awe when she met Leslie at their first meeting.

> Leslie and I had many things in common. First of all, her brother's name was Tim and that was the name of my son. Her brother had died from suicide after a long battle with alcohol and drugs. Leslie had been in recovery for twenty-eight years. We connected in so many ways. Then, all of a sudden, I noticed the cup Leslie was drinking from. It had words inscribed on it: "Hold on for one more day." I had not heard that song since 1991 when it came on the radio that day. That song changed my life. I couldn't believe it was coming back to me now. That same song, 'Hold On,' had cycled back into my life!

Carol eagerly expressed to Leslie how thrilled she was to see what was written on her cup. It was a sign, a reassuring blessing, encouraging her to open up and trust her. "Hold on for one more day" were words that had kept Carol dedicated to her recovery process, and now these words had even more meaning because they could be shared. In thoughtful detail, Carol told Leslie her story of that amazing moment in 1991 when the song came on the radio and stopped her from using again. Excitedly chiming in, Leslie shared her own story about the song. The amazing, synchronistic timing of this song's reappearance gave Carol a profound sense of safety, trust, and connection. Finally, the loneliness of stigma and shame had been eased by a shared moment of awe about a beloved song.

"I knew I was going to be okay. I felt so safe and so connected. Awe and wonder came back when we told our stories." It astonished Carol that so much meaning could be found in their awe-inspiring stories through the song.

"What was even more amazing was how it had been thirty-two years—like something really big had connected me to that song in 1991. And now that song had connected me to Leslie in 2023." The timing of these two events astounded her. "That song recycled back to me at the perfect time." Carol made the connection that "Hold on for one more day" for surviving her recovery from addiction was exactly the same message she needed for holding on through her grief.

What were the chances of this song coming back into her life at this time? It made her wonder—and it made her hopeful. Even if she could never figure out how this wondrous timing happened, there was an unshakable truth about these experiences of awe for Carol. "These awe moments always make me feel that I am going to be okay. It gives me a feeling of freedom. I feel lighter."

After that first connection with Leslie through the "Hold On" song, she continued to meet for counseling for several months. Eventually Carol began volunteer work for an affiliated organization, SADOD

(Support After a Death by Overdose), working to organize a peer grief conference.

One of the greatest benefits of volunteering for SADOD and going to support groups at the Sun Will Rise Foundation was joining in opportunities to share stories of awe and wonder with other peers. Carol enthusiastically encouraged other grieving people to share their stories of moments that took their breath away.

"Sharing awe through stories is the extra gift that comes back to me. I believe in the magic of listening to people's stories of wonder. The healing is in the listening." After telling her story to Leslie about her awe-inspiring event with the "Hold On" song, she was confident that sharing moments of awe with other survivors opened groups to meaningful moments of chills, goosebumps, insights, new perspectives, and deeper connections. "It is so mystical how awe works. People love to talk about it. It doesn't have to be a big thing. It can just be those little moments that make you wonder."

She recently rediscovered a few more awe and wonder moments that she had forgotten for decades. One of those recollections is from the age of thirteen. She recalls being at home, sitting on a wooden chair built into a small table—a telephone table commonly used for rotary phones in the late 1960s.

> I started carving with a pen the shape of a heart into the wood. Inside the heart, I wrote my name with an imaginary name of a boy. I carved "Carol and Jeff" into the heart. For some reason, my mom looked confused—and asked me why I'd written "Jeff" and not the name of my actual boyfriend at the time. I told her I had no idea why I wrote "Jeff." I didn't even know anyone named Jeff. And

for some mysterious reason, a man named Jeff ended up being my husband two decades later. I still cannot believe I wrote his name in that heart so long ago.

She wonders about other moments of awe, more recently. She had just received news about upcoming neurosurgery for her neck. At home, she worried alone at night. She asked Jeff in spirit to help her with the anxiety of her procedure.

I just needed a sign he was with me. I said to him, "I hope you stay with me through this." And I noticed suddenly that the digital cable clock said 11:11. It was a sign from him that everything was going to be okay. He used to send me texts letting me know it was 11:11 as a way of letting me know he was thinking about me. I checked my phone and saw seventeen text messages that said 11:11 from him over the past years. I know there are lots of explanations for this kind of 11:11 thing to happen, but the timing of seeing the 11:11 was reassuring for me at that moment. And it felt good to see his seventeen messages! These little signs do make me feel awe—and I feel better because I know I'm going to be okay.

Carol believes the healing power of awe and wonder comes from being open-minded and curious. Moments of awe can come to us anywhere and at any time. "Awe is everywhere in life. It comes to me when I need it—if I am open to it. I'm not afraid of it."

She feels the experience of awe is "a mystical way things happen that show you the light. It is a clear connection to something that gives you goosebumps. It's a powerful thing to get those goosebumps—so pay attention when that happens!"

The Healing Power of Sharing Awe with Others

Carol enthusiastically celebrates moments of awe in her healing process with others. Through her ability to listen closely and empathize, she encourages survivors of grief, trauma, and addiction to tell their stories of awe and wonder in unhurried, rich detail. In support groups, her deep listening and attunement to others allow participants to honor and reclaim their experiences. She recognizes our sense of wonder as a beacon of hope that gives us faith in the human spirit and humanity.

Her openness and passion for sharing awe and wonder stories with groups demonstrates how our private, personal experiences of awe can be even more meaningful when others hear them. Carol believes that sharing breathtaking moments of awe helps to break through the isolation of stigma and shame that comes with the grief of losing a loved one to an overdose. She recognizes how we feel "safe and connected" when an awe experience is shared, inviting others to be vulnerable and open, willing to "go there" with that person's awe moment.

Carol's rewarding experiences of connecting with Leslie and support groups through her stories of awe reveal the prosocial benefits of awe in healing from grief, stigma, disconnection, and shame. Neuroscience consistently shows how a shared moment of awe and wonder encourages people to be more vulnerable, open, curious, and humble. For example, consider the 2023 study "When Awe Strikes: The Ebb of Loneliness in Response to Awe and Human

Connection,"[1] or "Awe and the interconnected self," a study published in the *Journal of Positive Psychology* in 2021, or "Awe as a pathway to mental and physical health," APA Psych Net, March 2023.[2]

I have observed Carol in action sharing stories of "moments that take your breath away." When she tells her stories, the group's rapt attention and connection are palpable—the sense of belonging and oneness, being fully present, feeling goosebumps together, a gasp together, genuine curiosity, and a sense of time standing still.

Carol's sharing moments of awe with Leslie and later sharing stories with support group participants has strengthened her hope, resilience, and sense of community.

But after Jeff's death, before her breakthrough with Leslie, Carol suffered a particularly isolating type of grief that was difficult to share. She felt guarded about his death partly due to the stigma about his fentanyl overdose, which complicated her grief and intensified her loneliness.

Certain experiences of grief are risky to share because of stigma, fear of social judgment, criticism, or shame. This grief is not only awkward or unpleasant to talk about, but it can also be a risk to one's reputation, a taboo, or a topic to be avoided. It is a disenfranchised grief experience. Disenfranchised grief is a term coined in 1989 by grief researcher Kenneth Doka in his groundbreaking book, *Disenfranchised Grief: Recognizing Hidden Sorrow*. He defines disenfranchised grief "as grief that results when a person experiences a significant loss and the resultant grief is not openly acknowledged, socially validated, or publicly mourned."[3]

One of the greatest causes of loneliness is grieving something that no one seems to understand or appreciate. We silently suffer a loss because others have discouraged us from drawing attention to it. This is a grief we hide. It is our own private sorrow—unshareable—yet somehow bearable.

Carol was struggling to live with disenfranchised grief and bravely tried going to a support group to open herself to other people grieving the same tragedy of overdose due to substance use. She was attempting to find a way to heal the disenfranchised grief by *enfranchising* her experience with others who could understand and accept her. According to Kenneth Doka's approach to healing disenfranchised grief, we have a right to name our grief, to claim it rather than shame it. We can compassionately enfranchise our pain by befriending it, honoring it, and allowing our emotions to tell the truth—together with a group of people who have also been through the same struggle with stigma and shame.

Carol's willingness to share her story of awe with Leslie about the "Hold On" song on the radio was a breakthrough out of disenfranchised grief. This story of awe has been a pathway to enfranchising her grief—instead of hiding her pain. Sharing her awe is a way to share her grief, allowing her grief to be claimed, liberated, and validated. Indeed, according to the *Merriam-Webster Dictionary*, to "enfranchise" something or someone does mean to "set free."

I am moved by her faith in the healing power of awe as well as her faith in the healing power of sharing our stories—and group experiences of moments that take our breath away. Her stories and her activism with groups have revealed how our experiences of awe are not just for ourselves and our own personal well-being. These experiences offer more than material for self-improvement and personal growth because awe and wonder go beyond ourselves as a self-transcending emotion. Sharing our awe moments gives survivors of grief, trauma, and addiction a way to transcend ourselves through *each other's* amazement—drawing out the best in ourselves.

Whether group participants tell stories of visitations by sparrows, or waking up from a dream with an epiphany, or watching a solar eclipse, or of the divine timing of a song that blasted on the radio, people are hungry for meaning, validation, and celebration of wondrous moments. Our awe-inspiring stories can break us out of disenfranchised grief by enfranchising our ever-hopeful, ever-curious sense of wonder.

I am in awe of Carol and her vibrant sense of wonder. She emanates a warm sense of curiosity and openness—and it gives her a youthful glow. She would pause for a wondrous moment and notice a sign, or a nudge, or a beautiful, fleeting, perfect little miracle. As she attests, "Wonder is everywhere if you are willing to see it."

Carol's Wonder Wisdom in a Nutshell

What causes people to lose their sense of wonder?

Society can be harsh and judgmental.
Social pressure to fit in can push us away from our sense of wonder.

What helps trauma survivors heal through wonder?

Sharing our stories of wonder with each other.
Talking to people who have been through what you have.
We can inspire wonder in each other by showing interest.

Why are wonder and awe important for living in these times?

Wonder helps us stay authentic in a world of social pressure to be someone else.

Wonder helps us be honest with each other.

What is your favorite wondrous quote?

"Hold on for one more day.
—Wilson Phillips, "Hold On"

What wondrous book(s) do you recommend?

Living Clean: The Journey Continues by Narcotics Anonymous

What wondrous movie or video do you recommend?

Flashdance

What wondrous music or song do you recommend?

Richard Marx, all of his music, especially "Children of the Night"

The most awe-inspiring person you know (role models of openly wondrous and joyous behaviors)

My recovery sponsor, Laurie Nunes

Notes

1 Elias, H., Trujillo, A., & Claypool, H. (2023). When awe strikes: The ebb of loneliness in response to awe and human connection. *Journal of Student Research, 12*(2). https://doi.org/10.47611/jsr.v12i2.1932.

2 Monroy, M., & Keltner, D. (2022). Awe as a pathway to mental and physical health. *Perspectives on Psychological Science, 18*(1). https://doi.org/10.1177/17456916221094856.

3 Doka, K. J. (2008). Disenfranchised grief in historical and cultural perspective. In M. S. Stroebe, R. O. Hansson, H. Schut, & W. Stroebe (Eds.), *Handbook of bereavement research and practice: Advances in theory and intervention* (pp. 223–240). American Psychological Association.

8

Ricky Allen
The Awe-Inspiring Kindness of a Stranger

She gave me a second chance to change my life.

Ricky Allen is an inspirational speaker and mental health peer mentor who has presented for NAMI (National Alliance on Mental Illness) in Austin, Texas.

Ricky's Story

Born in 1991 in Missouri City, a suburb of Houston, Ricky was raised by Christian missionaries in an African American household. Proud to be helpful as the oldest of three children, he watched over his siblings as the "man of the house" while his father worked long hours as a plumber.

He describes his years in the Missouri City area up to the age of eight:

> Even though we were a low-income household in those years, we were a loving, resourceful family, and our parents took good care of us. There was always food on the table, and we all sat down together at meals. My parents taught us how to be responsible but also let us just be kids and be able to have fun. I had lots of neighborhood friends who played in our house with me and my brother and sister. We loved to play hide-and-seek in the house and other games.

After the family relocated to Lubbock in western Texas when Ricky was in the third grade, he faced racism and bullying in his school, unlike what he had experienced at his school in Missouri City.

> Fortunately, as a big kid for my age, I was introduced to football. Being on that team and playing as a lineman helped me deal with the racist attitudes at the school. But it was also a good outlet for me to express myself. Sports helped me learn to regulate my emotions and handle stress. Also, my family was very close and supportive, and protected us from the racism outside the home. But even though I played football, I stayed at home a lot because the neighborhood was not friendly. I played video games all through elementary school, middle school, and high school.

In 2003, at the age of twelve, after his mother had received her master's degree and was offered a job in San Angelo, the family relocated again. Ricky continued to excel at football and enjoyed the middle school friends who came to his home to play video games. He remembers these years as a happy and social period.

> My friends came from all walks of life. We really had a good time playing Halo on game nights. In those years, my parents became more involved with ministry work, and they spent more time outside of the home. I kept playing football and still loved it. Then in 2006, we had to move again to Austin, because the ministry work was important, and my parents had more responsibility in their roles.

By the age of sixteen, Ricky was forced to stop playing football due to an injury to his left shoulder. The loss of this vital role in his life left him feeling depressed and empty. He stayed home playing video games, gaining weight and becoming more lethargic and withdrawn. He continued to go to classes in high school, though his grades suddenly plummeted. Ricky remembers his first schizophrenia symptoms—hearing voices and hallucinations—appearing when he was alone at home.

> I heard voices—and I was not in control. I first noticed a voice talking to me when I was alone in the backyard at my house. It said, "It's a beautiful day." I answered out loud, "Yes, it is." I will never forget that first time talking with my first voice. But two more voices started to come in over the months—so there were three voices in total, two male and one female. I could not focus on my family members when they talked to me. My parents thought I was just zoning out and up in my head in my own little imagination. I also could not focus in the classroom. I became paranoid and

> kept worrying that someone was going to find out about my voices and put me in a mental hospital somewhere. I was afraid people in white coats would lock me up, like I had seen in the movies. Then I started skipping classes in my junior year of high school. And I started doing drugs, a lot of weed, and drinking alcohol. And believe it or not, I used LSD and other psychedelics. I mistakenly thought that using the drugs would help to control the symptoms of hearing voices and feeling depressed, but of course they made everything worse.

Ricky developed friendships with classmates and neighbors who joined him in increased drug and alcohol use. He received his high school diploma in 2009, but by then he admitted he had lost interest in starting a career and felt aimless, frustrated, and ashamed of his lack of focus. His symptoms progressively caused him to isolate himself, and he could only handle part-time retail jobs.

> I worked at Dollar General and Target—a lot of jobs. I even worked as my father's apprentice as a plumber. Between 2009 and 2012, I was really going through the wringer and getting progressively more depressed and isolated. I started self-mutilation, cutting myself on my arms and feeling a lot of shame. But I told no one, and covered up my scars, and that isolated me more. I just could not tell anyone about the voices and hallucinations because of stigma. (I understand now but didn't understand it at that time.) It was too much of a risk to let out my secret, and I could not bring shame to our strong, successful family. Being an African American male, I had to be cautious about how I expressed my emotions, so I had to hold back.

But Ricky was not aware he had schizophrenia and had no context for identifying his symptoms. At this time, he had not been diagnosed or evaluated. His symptoms frightened him, but he was able to put himself, as he describes, into "autopilot." He found music to be his favorite remedy for his bouts of paranoia. "Besides rock and hip-hop, I loved music from the 1970s! Earth, Wind, and Fire and so much great music got me through those years."

Ricky had a particularly close friend who enjoyed the same music and played video games with him. But one night in 2012, he heard the shocking news of his friend's suicide.

In his grief, Ricky did not eat or sleep for forty-eight hours. And worse, he heard harsh inner voices nagging him to drive immediately to his friend's gravesite in San Angelo. Exhausted and guilt-ridden by a sense of not being supportive enough or "there for my friend," Ricky broke down and gave in to the voices. He jumped into his car at midnight and drove 220 miles to his friend's gravesite in San Angelo, arriving at the cemetery.

> But the gate was locked—the gate would not budge. I could not get through to go see my friend's grave. I was so upset. I sat in my car for hours and saw hallucinations all around me. Another voice told me to drive further up to Dallas to visit my friend's family. I cared about his parents and thought I should go see them, but of course I was in no shape to be driving. I did not think about taking care of myself.

Ricky managed to drive towards Dallas for a few miles on the interstate in heavy morning traffic, but somehow he blacked out and he found himself in a car crash.

> Four eighteen-wheelers flew past me. Somehow I had skidded off the highway and I could see a jeep, pulled over in the left lane, that had been rear-ended by my car. Smoke was coming out of the hood of my car. I was in shock.

Ricky couldn't move and could not tell if he had been injured. A middle-aged woman with blonde hair, wearing a gray sweatshirt and jeans, stepped out of the jeep and walked over to his car with a genuine look of concern for him.

> She asked me, "Are you okay?" And I didn't know what to say. I felt terrible for hitting her jeep, but I wasn't exactly sure what had happened. She looked at me, and I felt ashamed because I expected her to be angry—yes, I had messed up and I was to blame for hitting her jeep, but she looked at me with so much kindness. She wanted to calm me down, just by standing by me, caring for me, as if she was my mother. She said, "The ambulance is on the way." I could not talk but I could see she knew I was in shock. It was like she was able to understand me, read my mind without speaking. I almost thought I was seeing an angel because she was so caring. She wanted to protect me.

Ricky was approached and briefly evaluated by the EMS workers from the ambulance that soon arrived, but he signed a waiver not to go to the hospital. He did not believe he was injured. He recalls that the woman returned to her jeep and left after the ambulance had left. He believes she never told him her name.

After checking his car, Ricky decided that he would try to drive back to Austin despite the damage, and fortunately, amazingly, he did manage to reach his home safely without any more problems.

As he rested quietly at home in his room that day, he realized how profoundly moved and amazed he was by the woman's kindness and caring. He felt it was a miracle that she had appeared at this time in his life, after the death of his friend, amid his illness and grief. He reflected on her words, "Are you okay?" and recognized how important it was to take responsibility for himself and to take care of himself. Caring mattered, and his self-care was part of caring for others. It was time to be honest with his family and ask for help.

> She gave me a second chance. She gave me a gift. She could easily have pressed charges. She didn't even file a claim. She didn't judge me or care what kind of background I had. She only wanted to help. She gave me a pass and the opportunity for a whole new life. I was blessed, but I also knew it was time to take responsibility for my illness and admit this to my family.

Just hours later, on the same day of the accident, Ricky told his parents about his ordeal with hearing voices, seeing hallucinations, battling substance use, depression, anxiety, the suicide of his friend, and the demolition of the car. "I told them *everything*—I completely opened up. I felt I should come clean to my family after that amazing miracle happened to me with a stranger on the highway."

Soon Ricky was evaluated at a psychiatric hospital during a nine-day stay. He was diagnosed with schizophrenia, depression, and anxiety and was prescribed medications. He underwent four other hospitalizations during the next few years, and his parents became active members of a support group for families as well as mental health advocates through NAMI (National Alliance on Mental Illness) at his local Austin chapter.

My parents and siblings are glad to be connected with NAMI. They wanted support and education to learn more about schizophrenia and how they could support me. I'm so relieved and grateful they became involved. No one in my family had ever known how to deal with schizophrenia. Education and awareness about mental illness gave our family a chance to be vulnerable and honest so we could help each other. It is so important that people know how to recognize and respond to the symptoms that affect teens and young adults.

A Second Chance Put into Action

Heartened by the support from his family, his peers, his local community, NAMI, and other mental health providers, Ricky moved forward with a solid commitment to his recovery.

But it was his profound, awe-inspiring connection with the woman in the accident that turned his life around, motivating him to take responsibility for his recovery. Ever since that life-changing moment, believing he was given a second chance by her act of kindness, he serves others by putting his second chance into action. He shows others who live with mental illness how to find hope, meaning, and purpose in their recovery.

He attended Austin Community College between 2016 and 2019 and earned an associate's degree in creative writing. During that time, he was awarded a certificate by NAMI for being a presenter for their series "In Our Own Voice: Living with Mental Illness."

Later in 2023, he appeared in a video series called *The Unfixed Mind: Navigating Mental Health Today*, produced and directed through a collaboration with Unfixed Media and the Health Story Collaborative. As an inspiring speaker, storyteller, mentor, and advocate, Ricky currently works full-time as a peer mentor for a community services agency in Austin, helping other young adults live with a mental illness.

> I like giving guidance and hope to peers going through the same struggles. I tell people all the time how grateful I am that I found the help I needed by opening up and being honest about what I was coping with. I also tell everyone that I think it is a miracle that I am still here. The woman in the accident who asked, "Are you okay?" has inspired my work. When I check in with people, I ask, "Are you okay?" every day. I carry on her message of kindness and caring.

In a video for *The Unfixed Mind* series, Ricky described a profound moment when a parent of someone he mentored expressed their appreciation for his work, calling him a hero. He broke into tears of gratitude and humility, realizing that he had truly given someone who had suffered like him a second chance.

His mission to pay it forward to his family and community continues today. "People need people in their lives to care enough to ask, 'Are you okay?' and to give each other a chance to be vulnerable. To be open and honest. Showing we care, human to human, can save a life."

How Awe Inspires Us to Care for Others

Awe can happen in our most vulnerable times. An amazing encounter can occur when we least expect it. We may be gripped in the throes of raw grief, or bitter shame, or bullying voices in our mind, but suddenly everything stops, and we are stunned by something that takes our breath away.

Ricky was extremely vulnerable and in grave danger when an unknown woman appeared from the smoke and chaos of the accident to check on him. Her genuine caring to ask him, "Are you okay?" was a brief, fleeting instant of awe that transformed his entire life and may even have saved his life. He will be forever in awe of this kind stranger who miraculously appeared to him. He still wonders if she could have been his guardian angel.

Up to that point, for six years, Ricky had been suffering from a terrible sense of shame about his mental illness, substance use, self-mutilating behaviors, depression, and anxiety, long before he was ever diagnosed with schizophrenia. The voices in his head, along with his self-loathing and grief over the suicide of his friend, overwhelmed him on the day of the accident. But somehow, the warm, reassuring voice of the woman resounded stronger than the other clamoring voices in his mind. Standing out from the others, her clear and gentle voice brought Ricky back to his senses, back to his body, and back to his awareness of where he belonged in the world—his family at home.

Amazingly, Ricky's awe experience lifted him out of his nagging, bullying thoughts and opened him to a kind, compassionate voice calling out to him. One fleeting moment of awe turned his shaming thoughts into kind thoughts—and turned his life around.

How did this happen?

As neuroscientists have consistently demonstrated, awe shifts us out of the default mode network of our brain (DMN) to bring our focus outwards to a new experience rather than inward to our thoughts. This means awe shifts us out of self-referential thinking (habitual thoughts about ourselves that cycle over and over) and out of our predictive coding (what we think will happen next) into just being present without "the baggage" of controlling thought patterns.

Metaphorically speaking, awe gives us a second chance to perceive reality without the baggage of controlling thoughts that bog us down. Instead of being hung up on our thoughts, we notice who is standing next to us. We listen better, we tune in, we watch closely, and care about something beyond ourselves. This outward shift is so powerful that we can see the world more objectively and observe people without as much bias or projection.

Ricky's experience demonstrates how a moment of awe can give us a second chance—and even give our own sense of self a second chance. His awe experience transcended his sense of self, from a chronically shaming and self-loathing self to a kind, compassionate self.

His moment with the woman allowed him to receive the gift of a second chance to live his life with kindness and compassion.

Amazingly, Ricky felt guided to take social action after this experience. He wanted to be present to others as the woman in the accident had been for him, with a nonjudging, nurturing approach to caring. "Are you okay?" became a guiding message for him, to care about others as well as himself. This became his mission to serve as an inspirational speaker, advocate, and mentor to others in recovery.

Many studies over the past ten years have shown that experiences of awe often lead people to want to help others in significant ways, such as through volunteering, community action, or simple acts of kindness. For example, the study "The Relationship Between Awe and Prosocial Behavior: A Three-Level Meta Analysis" (2024) shows us that awe experiences definitely spark an interest in volunteering or sharing with others.[1]

Another study in 2022, based on longitudinal surveys from 676 Chinese college students, demonstrated that awe was positively associated with prosocial behavior. The researchers reported, "Self-transcendental emotions, including awe, can lead to reduced self-attention and increased prosocial behavior" ("Awe and Prosocial Behavior: The Mediating Role of Presence of Meaning in Life and the Moderating Role of Perceived Social Support").[2]

A powerful experience of awe can spark a calling, a passion, or a mission, not only to change ourselves but to change the ways we interact with others.

Ricky's story inspires me to marvel at how a moment of awe so beautifully proves to us that we are not alone and not stuck forever in our heads. Something surprising and glorious can break through the isolation of shame, self-loathing, and fear—a caring voice, a song on the radio, a blue heron, a dragonfly. And after this breakthrough, we can see each other and hear each other with less baggage (of nagging thoughts) in the way.

Ricky's Wonder Wisdom in a Nutshell

What causes people to lose their sense of wonder?

Giving in to your own inner critic
Shame, fear, hopelessness

What helps trauma survivors heal through wonder?

Find a person who has a sense of wonder and listen to their story.
Share your story of wonder with someone you trust.

Why are wonder and awe important for living in these times?

Wonder is a motivator and gives us hope.
Wonder lets you know what matters to you.

What is your favorite wondrous quote?

Impossible is just a big word thrown around by small men who find it easier to live in the world they've been given than to explore the power they have to change it.

—MUHAMMAD ALI

What wondrous movie(s) or video do you recommend?

Interstellar
A Beautiful Mind

What wondrous music or song do you recommend?
"Drown" by Bring Me to the Horizon

Who are some awe-inspiring celebrities/famous people who are role models of openly wondrous and joyous behaviors?

Tim Duncan of the San Antonio Spurs
Denzel Washington

Notes

1 Gao, M., Qiu, X., & Zhu, H. (2024). The relationship between awe and prosocial behavior: A three-level meta-analysis. *Basic and Applied Social Psychology*, 1–15. https://doi.org/10.1080/01973533.2024.2433721.

2 Fu, Y. N., Feng, R., Liu, Q., He, Y., Turel, O., Zhang, S., & He, Q. (2022). Awe and prosocial behavior: The mediating role of presence of meaning in life and the moderating role of perceived social support. *International Journal of Environmental Research and Public Health*, *19*(11), 6466. https://doi.org/10.3390/ijerph19116466.

PART III

THE HEALING POWER OF AWE AND WONDER

Opening to Wonder: An Invitation

Learning from the perspectives of Robyn, Luke, Carol, and Ricky, I can better understand how awe and wonder heal us as survivors of trauma, loss, and addiction. I can recognize and marvel at how their wondrous experiences transformed their lives as well as transcended their own sense of themselves—and they all parallel my own journey in the following ways:

- Awe and wonder helped us to break through the stigma, shame, and isolation of our ordeals (such as being the victim of abuse, or surviving our child's death from an overdose, or struggling with a severe mental illness).

- Our awe and wonder experiences were only brief, fleeting moments, but they profoundly changed us (such as Robyn's few minutes with a dragonfly, Ricky's brief encounter of kindness from a stranger, or Carol hearing a song on the radio).

- Our awe and wonder experiences opened us to a sense of connection, community, and a desire to share our wonder.

- We all tapped our innate quality of openness that allowed us to expand our interests and curiosity for more experiences of wonder. In other words, once we experienced the power of wonder, we wanted to seek *more*—as a "wonder chaser," as Robyn described herself. Luke found wonder in everyday conversations and songwriting—and now regularly interviews people for a recovery newsletter. A wonderful listener with an open mind, he loves learning from other perspectives.

Indeed, that quality of openness is particularly vital for inviting awe and wonder experiences into our lives. Consider what Monica Parker observes in her book *The Power of Wonder: The Extraordinary Emotion That Will Change the Way You Live, Learn, and Lead*. "So, what kind of mindset makes someone wonder-prone? People who are present, open, mentally nimble, and curious about new ideas, people, and things in a deep and exploratory way."

Another delightful description for a wonder seeker (or wonder-prone person) comes from a book by Andrea Scher, *Wonder Seeker: 52 Ways to Wake Up Your Creativity and Find Your Joy*. She invites us to be wonder seekers with her uplifting definition. "Wonder Seeker: 1. Someone who actively looks for things that delight them. 2. A person who is curious and inspired, vibrant, and open-hearted."

It's heartening to claim that even one awe-inspiring moment that took our breath away could spark a lifelong love of learning and exploring, as well as a sense of purpose and belonging in the world. In the following chapter, we will take a wide, vast tour of the many worlds of wonder that beckon us to explore—with our exquisitely keen five senses. And perhaps, we can invite our wondrous side to be a wonder seeker.

9

Bringing Awe and Wonder into Our Lives

> *Three things remain with us from paradise: stars, flowers, and children.*
> —DANTE ALIGHIERI

Protecting Our Sense of Wonder in a Cynical World

Our experiences of awe and wonder can come to us in many ways—as a pleasant surprise when a cardinal lands near our window, or as a life-changing realization waking up from a vivid dream. We may have encountered awe-filled moments that took our breath away and eased our loneliness or anxiety, but too often we forget about them as we forge ahead in our daily realities. Many of us might not recognize how wonder restores us because these moments are underappreciated, unexplored, or tucked away.

Entire worlds of wonder are waiting for our discovery when we consider all the ways we have found wondrous things in the past. We probably already have a few favorite awe-inspiring interests and activities—our repositories of wondrous things to restore us.

But as easy and uplifting as restoring wonder in our lives may seem, for troubling reasons we too often spend time instead on our phones and screens, doomscrolling or racing to keep up on ever-breaking bad news. In the past few years, I have needed to force myself away from my devices and just take a merciful pause to restore a moment of wonder in my day. It has become a conscious, highly intentional activity to take "awe moments" or "wonder walks" for my peace of mind.

It's troubling to realize that I have fallen into scrolling habits and hypervigilant phone-checking behaviors that interfere with doing what I truly *want* to do with my day—including having a moment of wonder. To get through an especially rough day, I automatically jump on social media to distract myself from my worries and overwhelming responsibilities. Then I get sucked in and start feeling guilty and pissed off at myself for my lack of focus or self-discipline.

But I know it is much kinder and fairer to give myself a "wonder break." Instead of picking up my phone (again), I could take a couple of minutes to stop everything and just plop down by my window and watch the blue jays or chickadees hopping near me in the maple and oak trees. I am well aware, as a survivor of trauma and many losses, that these moments of awe are not simply nice little stress reducers—they are essential for my resilience. *And for me, my resilience is my resistance*—to the world's influences of cynicism, violence, exploitation, injustice, narcissistic and sociopathic abuse, fear-mongering, and so much more.

Our everyday sense of wonder is our strength, our protection, and our personal resistance to the outside forces that can dismiss and diminish the best parts of ourselves. Preserving our everyday sense of wonder can simply mean getting off our screens and stepping wholeheartedly into the day with a willingness to be amazed—at least not giving up on the wondrous person we are!

In his book *Stolen Focus: Why You Can't Pay Attention—and How to Think Deeply Again*, Johann Hari writes with alarm and compassion that our lives are too toxically distracted by screens, scrolling, and social media. We have lost touch with the part of ourselves that loves to wonder, daydream, or ponder. He calls for us to protect our attention—to be mindful of what we give our attention to, and to take care of our attention by protecting it from habits that destroy our ability to focus. "And there are certain things you need to protect your attention from, because they will sicken or stunt it: too much speed, too much switching, too many stimuli, intrusive technology designed to hack and hook you, stress, exhaustion, processed food pumped with dyes that amp you up, polluted air."[1]

Indeed, I believe our sense of wonder is fundamental to our resilience from the distracting, toxic forces Johann Hari describes. Furthermore, our resilience through our sense of wonder is a path of resistance for survivors of trauma and loss to prevent being triggered or misguided by these imposing worlds on our screens. In short, we resist: We won't let our sense of wonder be starved by giving too much of our attention and time to things that *demand* 100 percent of ourselves.

As Rachel Carson in *The Sense of Wonder* heralded the power of wonder to save our planet and our future for humanity, we, as survivors of trauma and grief, can nurture, preserve, and protect our ability to feel these vital emotions. Otherwise, without our wonder-seeking selves alive and well, we become desensitized, dehumanized, debilitated beings with only our screens to turn to. And as a trauma survivor, I know how bad it feels when the algorithms have succeeded in sucking me in!

Next, I would like to explore a host of ways to bring awe and wonder into our daily lives to preserve, protect, and restore the best of ourselves.

The Worlds of Wonder Around Us

Given how vital it is for survivors of trauma and loss to restore our sense of wonder, I would like to introduce actionable and natural ways to tap into the wondrous domains around us.

A solid place to start exploring the various domains of wonder is to turn to Dacher Keltner's descriptions of the "eight wonders of life," which he inspirationally describes in his book *Awe: The New Science of Wonder and How It Can Transform Your Life*. He is the founder of the Greater Good Science Center, a professor of psychology at the University of California, Berkeley, and the author of six books. His identification of sources of wonder in our world is truly a gift.

As I delve into each of these realms of wonder, I offer my insight and suggestions while keeping in mind what is particularly helpful for survivors of trauma and loss.

In addition to Keltner's useful categories of eight wonders of life, I also would like to offer ideas for other sources of wonder, such as the wonder of poetry (later in this chapter). I believe there can be more than eight categories of ways to find wonder, although it helps to get on a solid footing by beginning with Keltner's identified realms of wonder, then later, adding more as we explore.

The Awe-Inspiring Acts of People (Moral Beauty)

We can be in awe of people and the amazing things they do. In times when we have lost faith in humanity, or lost faith in ourselves, it is downright marvelous to spot a human being doing something wonderful—or a group, a community, or even a nation of people reaching far beyond our expectations. Dacher Keltner's research has shown that moral beauty is what most people have found to be the greatest source of awe. He believes, "Exceptional virtue, character, and ability—moral beauty—operate according to a different aesthetic, one marked by a purity and goodness of intention and action, and moves us to awe."[2]

Our level of awe could range from admiration to astonishment to utter amazement. We feel awe when we see acts of kindness, courage, heroism, brilliance, and skill, as well as acts of determination to overcome obstacles (both inner and outer forces).

Simone Biles courageously faced the challenges of the Olympic competitions as well as her own personal struggles. I was awestruck by her brilliant performance at the 2024 Paris Olympics. I had popped into my local sports pub to watch her on a massive screen with the crowd, and the entire room was spellbound while she competed flawlessly on the vault.

A few years earlier, she had spoken openly about her battle with anxiety and her fear that the "twisties" would interfere and endanger her vault performance. She had shared in many interviews that she had been through intensive psychotherapy and medication to improve her mental health. And then, for the world to witness, she triumphed on all levels and won a gold medal for her vault competition—along with three other medals!

It is enormously healing for trauma survivors to recognize and marvel at others with mental health challenges who have learned how to live with resilience and determination. Fortunately, celebrities today are more open and forthright about their personal struggles with addiction, trauma, or grief, taking an advocacy role to help reduce stigma and judgment. We can be in awe of the ways people share their vulnerabilities and still serve as role models, living inspirational lives.

Below are a few ways we can find awe by marveling at moral beauty (and perhaps boost our faith in humanity):

- Watching documentaries and biopic movies about inspiring people (*Lion, Hidden Figures, The King's Speech, Erin Brockovich, Nyad, Ray, Rocketman, An Angel at My Table, Seabiscuit*)

- Inspirational news stories (The Good News Network is a life-affirming publication of news stories about inspirational people and awesome acts.)

- Reading the memoirs of those who faced trauma and adversity (*I Know Why the Caged Bird Sings* by Maya Angelou, *What My Bones Know: A Memoir of Healing from Complex Trauma* by Stephanie Foo, *Angela's Ashes* by Frank McCourt, *Diary of a Young Girl* by Anne Frank)

- Poems that celebrate the wonders of the human spirit ("Amazement Awaits" by Maya Angelou, "The Power of a Circle" by Langston Hughes, "Songs of Togetherness" by Pablo Neruda)

- Interviews on talk shows with inspiring people (For example, actor Andrew Garfield talked openly with Stephen Colbert after the death of his mother, and the video of their conversation, "I hope this grief stays with me," is inspirational for facing loss.)

- Reading biographies of real-life heroes (*The Doctors Blackwell: How Two Pioneering Sisters Brought Medicine to Women and Women to Medicine* by Janice P. Nimura)

For more media resources and suggestions about moral beauty, see the "Friendly Guide to Wondrous Things."

Sharing Awe in Groups of People (Collective Effervescence)

We might remember a profoundly awe-inspiring gathering of people at an event such as a football game, a concert, a memorial service, or a dance festival. People move, sway, clap, chant, sing, or pray *in unison*, and we feel the convergence of the same emotions such as joy, ecstasy, reverence, or wonder (or other emotions such as grief, depending on the event). Just to be part of such an experience in person can bring goosebumps, induce chills, and take our breath away. People can light a candle or light their phones or wear lights to create a spectacular event with 30,000 in attendance at a concert or a memorial event. We can cheer for our team or sing at the top of our lungs. We can move our arms to create a wave that travels through a crowd the size of a city. The beauty of such an event is moving to witness, and so is the *contagion* of human emotions and movement.

There are also many ways to share collective effervescence in smaller groups. Recently, I attended a grief conference for people grieving the deaths of loved ones due to substance use. In a room of about twenty-five people, participants shared breathtaking accounts of awe moments that offered messages and guidance, as well as reassurance and love. The group members listened closely, with tears, or gasps, and chills of understanding. In these powerful moments of shared awe, we felt connected in unimaginable ways.

The following awe-inspiring activities can be remarkably meaningful for survivors of grief and trauma—and these can be applied in many healing settings:

- Sharing our own stories of wonder and awe with an appreciative group
- Watching a life-affirming movie (documentary) with a live, sympathetic audience
- Hearing an inspirational speaker share their passion for a cause at an event
- Attending a concert with songs that particularly move you as a survivor of grief
- Showing up to a vigil or candlelight event to honor loved ones or a cause
- Joining in a social action event for a cause you believe in

- Being part of an event for healing grief or a memorial gathering
- Being part of a support group where emotions are shared without judgment
- Reading a poem or inspirational literature out loud with an appreciative audience

For more examples and video/media suggestions for shared awe and wonder experiences, see the "Friendly Guide to Wondrous Things."

Nature: The Wonders of the Earth

The natural world offers endless ways to experience awe for many survivors of trauma and loss who regularly turn to wildlife for healing—as I do with my love of herons and their watery sanctuaries, and as Robyn encounters dragonflies. Even on solitary walks, we feel less lonely and enjoy our enchantment with the beauty around us.

When I work with seniors who have dementia, enthralling moments often happen outdoors just sitting by a tree and beholding the sights, sounds, and textures around us. One woman in an advanced stage of Alzheimer's loved to gaze upon the treetops as the breezes swirled through the branches and around her, and she laughed and swayed with the wind—pure wonder and joy!

To remember our awe experiences in nature, we can read exquisite poetry or novels that inspire our wonder of the natural world. We can also watch breathtaking videos and films that take us to foreign lands or the wonders of the universe through huge telescopes.

Here are some ways of bringing nature-oriented experiences of awe and wonder into our lives:

- Walking in nature ("awe walks")
- Forest bathing (the Japanese practice, shinrin-yoku, often involves two to four hours in nature)
- Quietly watching a sunrise or a sunset
- Watching birds (at a bird feeder, by a bird bath, or on trees near your home)
- Walking a dog or playing with a cat (We can also volunteer or work as dog walkers to enjoy the outdoors.)
- Volunteering for a wildlife or conservation organization
- Volunteering to teach children about wildlife at a school or science center
- Gardening and/or serving at a public garden
- Watching nature videos or documentaries and sharing these with others (*Yosemite HDII*, *The Octopus Teacher*, *Hidden Miracles of the Natural World*, *Winged Migration*)
- Watching the Webb Space Telescope online and sharing with others
- Exploring by bicycling, kayaking, canoeing, sailing, or just putting your feet in the water
- Gazing at the moon and the stars (especially if you can lie down on the ground on a warm summer night)

- Venturing off to a whole new country to see entirely different landscapes

For more examples of finding awe in nature, go to the "Friendly Guide for Wondrous Things."

Music

The wonderful thing about awe-inspiring music is how it quickly transforms and transports us without words, coaxing, or explanations. Music evoking vastness, openness, and mystery draws us in and takes us to other places—even in just seconds. Willingly and openly, we join the spellbinding journey, resonating, vibing, even floating with the melody, mood, and rhythms. The many genres of wondrous music provide a plentiful source of awe to nourish our souls.

Although our musical experiences today are brilliantly accessible through technology, nothing can top a live performance when we show up for an artist who has inspired us for years or decades. I'll never forget the chills of awe watching Sting singing *Synchronicity II* live, or *RiverDance* performed live in the 1990s, or the enchanting sound of flutes echoing across a pond at an outdoor concert much longer ago. These profoundly moving moments of live music permanently dwell in my soul, a wellspring of inspiration and wonderment—still showing up in my dreams decades later.

Music can take us to sublime states of awe where we open to spiritual awareness, such as when listening to Hildegarde Von Bingen's *Canticles of Ecstasy* from the year AD 1100. Or our hearts can soar while watching Coldplay perform "A Skyful of Stars" with an awe-filled audience of 40,000.

To my surprise and delight, I was awed watching a video of the Glastonbury Music Festival in England, where Coldplay's Chris Martin sang "Fix You" with Michael J. Fox, who has been suffering from Parkinson's disease for decades. The entire audience of thousands was moved, with many bursting into tears of awe and joy.

There will always be enthusiasts of dreamy, mystical, trippy, or sublime music, and as a lover of ethereal flow states, I would like to add more genres of awe-inspiring artists from other decades and centuries.

Awe-inspiring music might include works from:

- Celtic Woman, "The Voice"
- Hans Zimmer, Theme Song from *Interstellar*
- Enya, "Aniron" (Extended HD), "Only Time"
- Eric Whitacre, *Deep Field: Earth Choir*
- Blue Wave Studio, "Counting Galaxies"
- Coldplay, "A Skyful of Stars"
- Beach House, "Superstar"
- Moody Blues, "Your Wildest Dreams" or "Tuesday Afternoon"
- Ralph Vaughan Williams, *Fantasia on a Theme by Thomas Tallis*
- Gustav Holst, *The Planets* ("Neptune" is a classic far ahead of its time from 1917.)
- Joanne Shenandoah, "Peace and Power" or "Mother of Nations"

- Loreena McKennitt, "The Mystic's Dream"
- Jean Michel Jarre, *Oxygene II* (remastered from a gorgeous, trippy 1976 classic)
- Jon Anderson and Tangerine Dream "Loved by the Sun," from the *Legend* soundtrack
- Vangelis, "Antarctic Echoes," from the *Antarctica* soundtrack

For a more extensive list of music suggestions for inspiring awe and wonder, see the "Friendly Guide to Wondrous Things."

Visual Design (Sacred Geometries)

Art that inspires awe tends to be different from art that comforts or soothes us with familiar lines of beauty and harmony. Awe-enhancing art is more likely to evoke vastness and timelessness, and to take us beyond the familiar, often opening us to reach beyond our comfort zones. We may see beauty, yet in mysterious, unusual, or fascinating ways, outside of our expectations.

For example, the artist M. C. Escher stuns us with perplexing and intricate patterns and puzzles. Dreamy, otherworldly images by Freydoon Rassouli, William Blake, Rene Magritte, Chagall, or Odilon Redon draw us into fascinating new dimensions.

Museums offer "immersive" and interactive art experiences where we can wander amid astonishing projections of paintings and sculptures larger than imagined, captivating us with imaginative lighting. (For example, consider the worldwide immersive exhibit *Van Gogh: The Immersive Experience*.) Science museums display breathtaking visuals and show 3-D IMAX films that take us into space, deep into oceans, through time-lapse cinematography of growing microorganisms, or into spectacular ancient pyramids. Some museums feature optical illusions and technically fascinating new ways to see the world (such as the Museum of Illusions in Boston, New York, Seattle, Chicago, and 20 other US cities).

Cathedrals, castles, and palaces are popular places to find awe, of course. Included in the Seven Wonders of the World are amazing feats of architecture and engineering: the Great Wall of China, the Taj Mahal, Machu Picchu, the Pyramids of Giza, the Roman Colosseum, and more.

Even if we are not able to travel to exotic or enchanting destinations, we can enjoy virtual tours to explore them (such as those from the Smithsonian or the Metropolitan Museum of Art, or Tripsavvy tours). And of course, we can experience vast, immersive vistas with virtual reality headsets, goggles, and video games.

A few awe-inspiring visual experiences through film might include *Life of Pi, 2001: A Space Odyssey, Lawrence of Arabia, Interstellar, Arrival, The Tree of Life, Gravity, Bladerunner* (1982) and *Bladerunner 2049, Wicked, Close Encounters of the Third Kind, Spirited Away,* and *The Boy and the Heron.*

Spirituality and Religion

Most of us think of spirituality as a sense of connection to something larger than ourselves. In our experiences of awe, we feel a connection to something vast and incomprehensible. We later wonder about these extraordinary or stunning moments, seeking to find words and concepts to understand them. Awe is often a gateway to spirituality, of questing and wonder. We quest for meaning, purpose, belonging, or serenity. Many of us think of spiritual awe as mystical in nature.

Spiritual practices open us to everyday awe and wonder, and conversely, experiences of awe beckon us to appreciate more spirituality in our lives.

Spiritual awe, in terms of neuroscience, quiets our self-referential thinking and opens us to vast states of awareness and oneness with what is beyond ourselves. (The default mode network, DMN, of our brain circuitry is deactivated in a state of mystical awe, which allows our attention to go to what is outside of ourselves, rather than our own thoughts.)

According to Verywell Mind, "spirituality is a worldview that suggests a dimension to life beyond what we experience on the sensory or physical levels."[3] Spirituality is typically a personal, individual journey of discovery, spiritual growth, and finding wisdom.

In comparing religion to spirituality in terms of awe experiences, we can think of religion as an organized system of beliefs, values, practices, and rituals, expressed through religious traditions. The *Cambridge Dictionary* states that religion is "a belief in or worship of a god or gods, or any such system of belief and worship." People who worship through a religion find a sense of connection, comfort, and community, as well as a collective sense of awe (collective effervescence). Profound experiences of awe and wonder are shared when people come together for prayer, rituals, vigils, songs, chants, or sermons.

The religions of the world offer rich, well-established paths to awe, wonder, and reverence through a myriad of ways. According to the *World Atlas*, the largest religions worldwide are Christianity

(2.38 billion followers), Islam (1.90 billion), Hinduism (1.16 billion), Buddhism (506 million), Shinto (104 million), Sikhism (25 million), Judaism (14 million), Taoism (12 million), Confucianism (6 million), and Caodaism (4.4 million).[4]

Many survivors of trauma and loss combine personal spiritual practices alongside deeply held religious beliefs. Recently, a large Harvard study showed that including spirituality and religion in treating patients at medical centers was linked to better health outcomes. In their 2024 study, "Spirituality as a Determinant of Health: Emerging Policies, Practices, and Systems," the authors stated, "Spirituality includes a sense of ultimate meaning, purpose, transcendence, and connectedness." Given this understanding of spirituality, moments for spiritual practice, such as pausing to say a prayer, a blessing of thanks, or an affirmation, can be helpful by opening us to reverent states of awe and wonder.

People who practice spiritual or religious rituals are open to allowing a moment of awe—by inviting or invoking a state of attunement and reverence. These rituals can take place indoors or in nature, and alone or with others.

Following are some examples of common, actionable ways to bring awe and wonder into our day through spiritual practices and activities—even if we pause for just five minutes. These are popular activities that invite moments of awe that I have witnessed in my work as a rehabilitation counselor and as a grief support facilitator.

- **Expressing gratitude through blessings, prayers, or journaling.**

Pausing to be grateful, opening a space in our day to allow a moment of thanks creates an opportunity for awe and wonder.

If we want to deepen the practice of gratitude, we might turn to books of blessings such as Julia Cameron's *Blessings: Prayers and Declarations for a Heartful Life*, or John O'Donohue's *To Bless the Space Between Us: A Book of Blessings*, Jan Richardson's *The Cure for Sorrow: A Book of Blessings for Times of Grief*, or the ever-popular stories from *Chicken Soup for the Soul: Count Your Blessings*.

- **Centering ourselves with affirmations, prayers, devotionals, and mantras.**
Pausing to say an affirmation out loud is a way of opening ourselves to the wonders of the day. So is praying, singing, or chanting (such as the Buddhist mantra of Nam-myoho-renge-kio).

    Stopping the day for a few minutes to affirm the values that we are intentionally living is a spiritual practice in its own right. There are dozens of awe-inspiring books of affirmations for different groups of survivors and people in recovery, including *Morning Affirmations: 200 Phrases for an Intentional and Openhearted Start to Your Day* by Jennifer Williamson (who is a suicide loss survivor), or *Affirmations for the Inner Child* by Rokelle Lerner.

- **Reflecting or meditating on spiritual texts, teachings, or poems to evoke a sense of awe**
For thousands of years, contemplative and meditative practices have sprung from teachings and scriptures. Spiritually

inspiring words and phrases, even from poetry, can invite a profound moment of awe.

- **Noticing signs and synchronicities (and keeping a journal or log of these occurrences)**
  Opening ourselves to signs and synchronicities are popular spiritual practices for tapping mystical awe. We may be awed by the synchronicity of someone calling us when we are thinking about that person (especially if the call was unexpected, or we haven't seen that person in a while). We may notice a certain number that reappears at a particular time (such as 11:11 on our clock), a particularly meaningful song that suddenly comes on the radio (see Carol's story in Chapter 7), or a feather appears out of the blue. Many trauma and loss survivors attest that these signs and synchronicities represent divine timing in action—and find enormous relief and reassurance from these awe-filled moments. We feel that we are on the right track or that we are being guided or protected.

It is particularly meaningful and illuminating to keep a journal or log of these occurrences. I have worked with clients who find encouragement and guidance when they see patterns of signs and synchronicities unfolding in their daily lives. These brief, fleeting moments could easily be forgotten in the midst of a busy day, and yet later, as we review these little surprises—coincidences, synchronicities, nudges, "wow" moments—we can "connect the dots" and see a greater power at work beyond our own imagined outcomes.

When we keep a log of these moments and track them over days, weeks, or months, we can observe these seemingly random happenings and begin to see patterns, meanings, or a sense of guidance.

For a more spiritually oriented look at signs and synchronicities, the *New York Times* bestseller *Signs: The Secret Language of the Universe* by Laura Lynn Jackson is full of awe-inspiring stories. The highly popular series of "Godwink" books, *When God Winks: How the Power of Coincidence Guides Your Life* by Squire Rushnell, has introduced survivors of grief and loss to the wonders of signs, synchronicities, and divine timing. Integrating neuroscience and examining the role of signs, Tara Swart, MD, PhD, explores the power of wonder, openness, and intuition in her book, *The Signs: The New Science of How to Trust Your Instincts*. For a deeper dive into understanding synchronicity as well as Carl Jung's work, I recommend Jean Shinoda Bolen's *The Tao of Psychology: Synchronicity and the Self*.

- **Creating an altar or special spot such as a grotto, shelf, or small table for wondrous things—a feather, a seashell, an icon, a written prayer, an image, a candle**
  Quite simply, having a sense of appreciation and reverence for important, symbolic keepsakes can evoke moments of wonder. We can take a few minutes to sit by a sacred spot where we can reflect on symbolic and deeply meaningful objects that remind us of people, places, and things that inspire awe.

- **The act of beholding, gazing, and attunement**
  I would like to add a concept for spiritual practice called "beholding." It is a simple practice of pausing to deeply appreciate something that inspires awe (as I found by spending time beholding the blue herons). Most of us have favorite ways of beholding, such as gazing at ocean waves, or a sun setting behind the treetops, or watching a fire in the fireplace, a

burning candle, or sun beaming through a hanging crystal that makes prisms on your wall, even beholding a sleeping, purring cat (a spiritual practice in its own right!). Forest bathing is a beholding practice developed in the Japanese culture. And most of us love to simply sit on a porch or a balcony, beholding the beauty of the evening. Another version of beholding could be the spiritual practice known as gazing. Soul gazing (sitting with your partner and gazing into each other's eyes), candle gazing, sun gazing, mirror gazing, or star gazing are similarly wondrous activities for our spiritual nourishment.

It is helpful to remember the root meaning of the word *behold*, which means to "hold thoroughly with care" (from Old English, *bi* and *haldan*). By making time to hold space for what we love by the act of beholding, we can find everyday sources of awe. Perhaps this comes just from slowing down and looking up to what is around us (and off our screens). Theologian and author Matthew Fox writes about the practice of beholding: "Beholding implies respect and awe and wonder. Great mystics know a lot about beholding."[5]

- **Rituals to stay connected to deceased loved ones**
  We can create rituals to connect with our deceased loved ones through activities or routines, such as saying their name out loud, placing flowers on an altar, or adding photos at a special spot. By making dedicated times of the day sacred to remember our loved ones, we create moments for wonder as well as solace. (The Continuing Bonds Model of Grief, based on the work of Steven Klass, Dennis Nickman, and Phyllis

Silverman, offers psychological understanding and reassurance on healthy ways we can stay connected to our loved ones.)

- **Dreams**
  Sharing our dreams, studying their meanings and symbolism, and keeping a log of our dreams can offer fascinating moments of awe and wonder.

- **Totemic practices**
  Totemism is the belief in having kinship and spiritual relationships through animals, birds, plants, and other lifeforms on earth. Many of us find spiritual meaning and connection through totemic beliefs as we pause to recognize and appreciate our totem bird or animal, often with prayer, a blessing, or giving thanks.

For more on awe-inspiring spiritual and religious activities and media, see the "Friendly Guide to Wondrous Things."

Birth and Death

Most of us have experienced something wondrous, if not miraculous, when we have witnessed the birth or a death of a loved one. We marvel at an infant taking its first breath. Or we wonder about the final stages of dying. These life passages reveal the wonders of creation.

Women giving birth commonly experience a self-transcendent sensation of awe. A 2023 study, "Birthing as an experience of awe: Birthing consciousness and its long-term positive effects," reports, "Experiencing awe during birthing empowers women, thus promoting well-being in the challenging postpartum period."[6] Awe is a powerful emotion occurring during the birthing experience that is also shared by loved ones who are present at childbirth.

On the other end of the spectrum of life, an even greater amount of study has examined the awe experiences of dying.

Dr. Christopher Kerr, a palliative care physician who has worked with hundreds of dying people in hospice settings, states that most of his patients have seen visions before their death. More than 60 percent of these visions involve visits with loved ones who have died before them, providing a warm sense of comfort and welcoming.[7]

Studies of end-of-life experiences (ELEs) have become more common, thanks to the reporting of experiences of healthcare providers working in hospice and palliative care services. Normalizing the occurrences of ELEs helps to invite an open attitude to appreciating awe and wonder during the dying process.

Helping to advance our understanding of the phenomena that occur at the end of life, Dr. Kenneth Doka offers ways to perceive these awe-inspiring experiences through his practice as a psychologist as well as a minister, in his book, *When We Die: Extraordinary Experiences at Life's End*. He admits that a sense of mystery may be challenging for scientists to uphold but acknowledges that (even as a social scientist) he can stay open and hold contradictory experiences together to conceptualize inexplicable end-of-life experiences such as terminal lucidity. He encourages our ability to consider possible extraordinary (afterlife) connections with an open mind (a "maybe" approach), mixed with our logical explanations.

A particularly wondrous phenomenon, terminal lucidity, can occur when people with advanced stages of dementia unexpectedly and briefly return to a remarkably clear, lucid state of mind soon before their death. It's breathtakingly marvelous when someone with dementia who has become nonverbal and unresponsive for a year suddenly starts, for example, singing a pitch-perfect song from a favorite musical. It's as if that person comes alive from a younger chapter in life, animated and fully functioning. I've witnessed these phenomena on a few occasions with seniors with dementia in assisted living communities where I have provided recreational activities. Once, a woman, formerly an English teacher, completely nonverbal in her late stage of Alzheimer's, stood up proudly from her wheelchair and, in a lovely, clear voice, recited the entire Shakespeare Sonnet 116 ("Let me not to the marriage of true minds") in front of her daughter, granddaughter, and several staff members. We were moved to tears. It is as if this woman was leaving a message before her time to leave this earth. Two days later, indeed, she died.

I am still moved to tears when I remember how those tender, sacred minutes comforted that daughter and granddaughter who knew her soul so well as a lover of sonnets. I will always find terminal lucidity to be an utterly amazing phenomenon.

The study of near-death experiences is even more popular. The International Association for Near Death Studies (IANDS) provides extensive multidisciplinary research for NDE experiencers, healthcare professionals, educators, and researchers. This organization serves as a clearinghouse for finding classes, study groups, and resources for anyone interested in this fascinating topic.

My own NDE at age five when I nearly drowned has vividly stayed with me all my life, more lucid than a regular dream. I felt myself disappear into dense, brilliant light, which is a stunningly common characteristic of an NDE that neuroscientists are studying, often by examining the role of the default mode network (DMN) of the brain. In short, I left my body behind as some other part of my awareness rose up to the light. Similarly, people in different stages of dying often have powerful spiritual experiences.

Epiphany

An epiphany is a sudden realization that can transform our perspective and our lives. An epiphany moment can strike us out of the blue—while we are in the shower, watering our potted plants, or playing frisbee with our dog. Unexpectedly, out of nowhere, we have an "aha" experience that blows us away. Something amazing, maybe even miraculous, has "connected the dots" in our psyches, and we "get it!"

According to *Merriam-Webster*, an epiphany is "an intuitive grasp of reality through something (such as an event) usually simple and striking," and "an illuminating discovery, realization, or disclosure."

Personally, I resonate with the word "illuminating" for my own epiphanies, as a great deal of light is shed on a whole new realization. I have had a few powerful aha moments in my life, such as when a blue heron landed ten feet away from me. Those thirty seconds of that heron encounter did not simply transform me—it saved my life. Robyn experienced an epiphany with the dragonfly by her son's grave (see Chapter 5), beckoning her to turn her grief into purpose by helping others.

Dacher Keltner describes the wonder of epiphany in his findings from his studies with participants. "In each instance, the epiphany united facts, beliefs, values, intuitions, and images into a new system of understanding."[8] Amazingly, so many diverse faculties within our brains can suddenly all work *together* to create an epiphany—a lot going on in our brain at once!

Many survivors of trauma and loss have had wondrous moments of epiphany (aha moments) while writing in their journals and "connecting the dots" to notice patterns in their lives. It is exciting to look for patterns of personal growth with epiphanies and wonder how our lives have changed after each one.

We can consider some famous epiphanies to inspire us.

Famous Epiphanies in Literature

- Scrooge, in *A Christmas Carol*, woke up one morning as an entirely new (much kinder) person.
- Scout had an epiphany in *To Kill a Mockingbird* about her father's teachings of equality and kindness.
- In *The Crucible*, John Proctor had an epiphany that we will be forgiven by God.
- Jean Valjean, when he experienced an act of unexpected kindness from Bishop Myriel, had an epiphany in *Les Misérables*.

Famous Epiphanies in Real Life

- Isaac Newton had an epiphany about gravity when an apple fell on his head from a tree above him.
- Albert Einstein had a burst of insight about his theory of relativity when he came home tired one night.
- Mathematician Archimedes had an epiphany when determining the density of gold.

- Helen Keller, who was blind and deaf, had an epiphany with her tutor, Anne Sullivan, when she realized how to communicate through spelling "water" with her hands.

Activities to Cultivate Everyday Awe

In addition to the eight domains of wonder that we have explored, I would like to offer a few more wonder-enhancing activities.

- **Keep an awe portfolio, or a journal of awe and wonder moments.**
  Positive psychology researcher Barbara Frederickson recommends keeping a Positivity Portfolio to keep our favorite awe-inspiring images, photos, thoughts, quotes, poems, memorabilia, and other encouraging symbols.[9]

- **Create a playlist of awe-inspiring videos and music on YouTube or Spotify.**
  Having a dedicated playlist of awe-enhancing favorites is a wonderful way to give ourselves a well-deserved time out for wonder.

- **Enjoy wondrous poetry (to read alone or share aloud).**
  Engrossing ourselves in poetry can also include watching videos of poems being read by the poet or by other readers.
  Awe-inspiring videos with poetry include "Stopping by Woods on a Snowy Evening" by Robert Frost (various versions) and "Wild Geese" or "The Journey" by Mary Oliver (different versions including the poet reading her poems).

Here are a few poems that inspire wonder—and are wonderful to read aloud with others:

"The Peace of Wild Things" by Wendell Berry

"My Heart Leaps Up" and "I Wandered Lonely as a Cloud" by William Wordsworth

"The Ponds" and "Poem of the One World" by Mary Oliver

"Don't Go Back to Sleep" by Rumi

"A Brave and Startling Truth" by Maya Angelou

- **Write, blog, and share stories of your own personal experiences of awe and wonder.**
  Storytelling through writing, blogging, vlogging, or videos about our awe moments can open doors to wider connections with others and build community.

- **Travel, touring, exploring new places, near and far.**
  Transporting ourselves to undiscovered, new places, whether by car, by plane, by boat, by bicycle, or by walking, visiting other locations outside of our usual routines can open our eyes and our minds. Even in our own city or town, we might be a "tourist" and go to a local museum, art gallery, or a river park for the very first time.

For more ideas and resources for activities, see the "Friendly Guide to Wondrous Things."

Notes

1. Johann Hari, *Stolen Focus: Why You Can't Pay Attention—and How to Think Deeply Again* (New York: Crown, 2022), 273.

2. Dacher Keltner, *Awe: The New Science of Everyday Wonder and How It Can Transform Your Life* (New York: Penguin Books, 2023), 11.

3   Elizabeth Scott, PhD, "How spirituality can benefit your health and well-being," *Verywell Mind* (October 2, 2024).

4   "The 10 largest religions in the world," *World Atlas*, WorldAtlas.com, 2024.

5   Matthew Fox, "Learning to behold," *Daily Meditations with Matthew Fox* (May 30, 2024).

6   Dahan, O. (2023). Birthing as an experience of awe: Birthing consciousness and its long-term positive effects. *Journal of Theoretical and Philosophical Psychology*, 43(1), 16–30. https://doi.org/10.1037/teo0000214.

7   Alex Orlando, "Hospice physician shares insights on visions and near-death experiences," *Discover* (May 2, 2021).

8   Dacher Keltner, *Awe: The New Science of Everyday Wonder and How It Can Transform Your Life* (New York: Penguin Books, 2023), 18.

9   Barbara Frederickson, PhD, *Positivity: Top-Notch Research Reveals the 3-to-1 Ratio That Will Change Your Life* (New York: Harmony, 2009).

10

Resilience and Community Through Awe and Wonder

The world will never starve for want of wonders;
but only for want of wonder.
—G.K. CHESTERTON, *TREMENDOUS TRIFLES*

A Red-Tailed Hawk

One Sunday morning, I awoke at 4:30, irritated at myself for not being focused enough to meet a deadline for a blog post. Easily distracted and scatterbrained for two days, in fits and starts I had pushed myself to write and edit, but my painstakingly well-chosen words rubbed me the wrong way until I just deleted my work. My inner demons could not wait to pile on my pity party of angst that I couldn't get any work done. I was frozen and panicked that I could not function, although so much was depending on me.

I figured there must have been some underlying reason for my lack of focus. So, with my second cup of coffee, I sat down to figure out the cause of my poor concentration—but I couldn't concentrate well enough to explain the cause of my poor concentration! This attempt to analyze my headspace made everything worse, as my brain strained to handle conflicting topics fighting for my attention, as if too many tabs were open. After spending my seventieth birthday in the ER with a deep-vein blood clot in my leg the previous month, I could not afford $600 for a month's supply of blood-thinning medication—and I was furious at the price-gauging in our healthcare system. I was fearful after the US election that safety nets for struggling seniors would disintegrate. The world at the brink of more wars, famines, viruses, and climate disasters filled me with grief, and as I sighed, I teared up remembering a trusted colleague had just ghosted me. And to top it off, I was going to be alone for another effing Christmas holiday.

Doomful overthinking about my habit of overthinking was giving me another "bad head" day. I just could not focus! My thoughts jumped to the title of the book *Stolen Focus*, by Johann Hari, on why we cannot pay attention or think. What had stolen my focus? Was there just too damn much going on in my life and in this world these days? What was keeping me from concentrating—or was my own thought police coming after me? My PTSD symptoms were in full attack mode as my thoughts raced and darted about like frightened mice in a cage.

It was now only 7:30 on this cold, clear morning. I was so fed up with myself that for a quick distraction from my ugly, unbearable headspace, I jumped on TikTok and began scrolling through the "for you" videos. I viewed angry post-election conspiracy theories, drones (or UFOs) over New Jersey, MSNBC ratings dropping, H5N1 bird flu increasing, a CEO shooting, and nuclear doomsday threats.

After ten minutes of ugly, restless viewing, I turned off my phone. I was even more frustrated with myself, deciding that it was stupid of me to have watched that drivel.

I just wanted my thoughts to please quiet down and at least allow some peace. I stared out beyond the window to the bare branches of a row of oak trees against a deep blue sky. I sighed, just taking in the vivid blueness of the sky.

Then, flying out of the blue, a red-tailed hawk landed directly in front of me in the nearest tree. Awestruck, I held my breath. This bird stood still, staring in my direction for at least fifteen minutes as I stopped everything. My mind quieted in this rapt moment, my eyes fixed on its gaze. I marveled at the majesty of the hawk's sentinel stance with its deep reddish-brown wings and light cream down feathers.

Entranced for many minutes, I beheld the hawk in the oak tree on this glorious December morning. A strong, steady breeze blew across its feathers and rocked the branch on which it perched. Another, sharper breeze swirled down to the ground, scattering a few brown leaves over little patches of snow. The hawk didn't budge. I didn't move.

I hadn't felt this kind of awe in a long time, this quiet reverence and openness of spirit. I thought of my father's love of red-tailed hawks and wondered if his spirit had anything to do with this bird's bold arrival. I had never in my life seen a hawk so close that stayed for so many minutes.

So as not to disturb this bird, I slowly and carefully went to find the binoculars my father had given me twenty-three years ago, stored at the bottom of a set of drawers. I stealthily returned to the window to watch the hawk, which was still standing at the same spot. Through the binoculars, I saw in exquisite detail its full plumage and face, and determined that this bird did indeed have all the markings of a red-tailed hawk.

Delighted by the intricate, close-up views of the hawk through the binoculars, I expressed my thanks to my father out loud. I sweetly remembered his visit with me in Freeport, Maine, when he happily bought me the binoculars for my birthday. I remembered our walk in Wolfe's Neck Woods, mutually enthralled by our beloved birds, and how we both felt a sense of peace when he said, "Hawks are to me like your herons are to you."

How stunningly divine the timing was for this hawk to arrive this morning, when I was so starved for a moment of wonder—a way back to my soul. Through the enchantment of a hawk, I was released from the grip of my ruminating, destructive thoughts. I could still feel the magic I once knew back in the days I spent with the blue herons in their watery sanctuaries in Virginia and Maine. I reclaimed a profound, peaceful sense of connection with my father in spirit.

I also marveled at the symbolism of the binoculars my father had given me finally being put to good use after two decades lying at the bottom of a drawer. Why had I not used those binoculars to see wildlife around me for so long? Now, at last, I could see in more detail and take the time to see more. Even though I lived in a bustling neighborhood in Boston, Massachusetts, wildlife did indeed live here—and fared fairly well. Hawks and owls swooped down to the oaks, pines, and maple trees, and squirrels, blue jays, cardinals, robins, chickadees, seagulls, chipmunks, rabbits, crows, and woodchucks all thrived in well-tended gardens, yards, decks, and patios. Three houses down from me, at a Montessori school, small groups of children played and danced, and on winter days, I could hear joyous songs, rhymes, and games in action from inside the walls.

Metaphorically, the binoculars offered me a message to *deepen* my attention rather than scatter it. I needed to slow down and look deeper. I had missed noticing the intimate abundance and splendor of the details of my little routines. Most of all, I had missed appreciating the rich, deeper meanings of the web of life in my physical surroundings. After my hawk encounter, it occurred to me that survivors of trauma, with our hypervigilant imaginations and keen nervous systems, can find healing just by diving into rapturous moments with wondrous things around us. In short, with our extreme sensitivity, we are perfectly equipped to infuse ourselves with moments of awe. We are wired for awe and wonder—and responsive to those vast, sublime emotions.

Gosh, I thought, no wonder we feel so lonely, empty, and anxious so much of the time—we just do not allow ourselves to feel awe. We think we need some kind of big exotic vacation, or a spectacular celestial event, or an angel to visit us to give us magic. I thought I needed to travel back to the coast of Maine or Scotland to restore my sense of wonder—but this morning, wonder was right here.

By reflecting on my moment with the hawk, I wondered how fifteen minutes of awe had transformed my "bad head" day into a good day. How did that happen?

I decided to examine this healing encounter through the language of neuroscience. I wanted to create a checklist of what I had learned and compare it to the experience that had made me feel so much better.

Awe moments lift us out of the nagging thoughts, overthinking, and ruminations of our minds. When we are in awe, we stop trying to control and anticipate what will happen next ("predictive coding"). Awe pulls us into the present moment and turns our attention outside of ourselves, out of our self-referencing thinking, towards what is right in front of us.

Considering how awe deactivates the default mode of our brains that keeps our thoughts catastrophizing and jumping to conclusions, *we can give ourselves a break from that default headspace by giving ourselves a moment of awe and wonder.*

Dacher Keltner says this best: "How does awe transform us? By quieting the nagging, self-critical, overbearing, status-conscious voice of our self, or ego, and empowering us to collaborate, to open our minds to wonders, and to see the deep patterns of life."[1]

In a neuroscientific nutshell, here is what the brain is doing when we are experiencing a moment of awe—such as what I felt with the hawk:

- **The prefrontal cortex and anterior cingulate cortex are activated.** This means our executive function is activated and gives us the ability to focus and regulate our emotions.[2] *I can focus.*

- **The brain releases dopamine.** This neurotransmitter is associated with pleasure and reward, as well as balanced movement and coordination. *I feel better.*

- **Oxytocin is increased.** Instead of the fight-or-flight response, we switch to the "tend-and-befriend response" (a term coined by psychologist Shelley Taylor). This is our ability to connect with others to find support. Oxytocin activates a social response to stress. *I don't feel alone. I feel connected to my father in spirit.*

- **The vagal tone is increased.** This reduces stress and anxiety, including the allostatic load (the stress in the body that you accrue over time). The vagus nerve also regulates the release of pro-inflammatory cytokines that affect inflammation. Inflammation is lowered in the body. *I feel calm and grounded.*

- **The default mode network (DMN) is deactivated.** This switches us out of our self-referential or self-centered thinking to pay attention to what is outside of ourselves (including noticing other people and the greater surroundings). *I can get out of my head.*

A Willingness to Be Amazed

That day, I embraced my encounter with the hawk as a great, restorative blessing. It felt good, right down to my bones, to be grateful for the gifts of wonder.

If a few minutes with a hawk on a bright December morning could lift my spirit out of my default brain funk, I was truly thankful. I was grateful for the hawk's arrival, most definitely. But I was also thankful that I was *able* to feel awe. My entire body, mind, and soul needed that blast of awe and wonder. Somehow, I was able or open enough to allow myself to feel awe and wonder. It struck me that experiences of awe happen to us not only because of the source of the awe (a hawk, a heron, a dream), but also because of our ability to open to awe.

Or was it perhaps due more to our *willingness* to open to awe?

What makes us able to open to awe? What makes us willing to be amazed? Certainly, we cannot always count on a particular source of awe to come to us at will, and getting too attached to a given source of awe can have disappointing outcomes. We know wondrous things happen, but we cannot always make them happen. And yet we can claim and preserve our sense of wonder so that we are able and *willing* to experience an awe moment when it arrives. If we are open-minded about experiences giving us wonder, we are likely to find these moments more often—and the more we invite wonder into our daily lives, the easier it is to tap into our sense of wonder. It works both ways.

One of my favorite inspirations for opening myself to wonder is reading the poetry of Mary Oliver. A book of her poems, *Devotions*, has become a source of devotionals to spark my wondrous side.

If there is one survivor of trauma who transformed her life through awe and wonder, I would choose Mary Oliver as my shining example. In a 2011 interview in *O Magazine* conducted by Maria Shriver, Mary Oliver revealed that she had been sexually abused as a child.[3] I wondered if her love of nature began as a child and helped her survive her home life by finding safe places outdoors. I imagine she built little forts in the woods (as I did as a child) to spend hours away from home with her wildlife companions.

Her sense of belonging in the natural world is prevalent throughout four decades of her poetry. With her deep love and reverence for the earth, her passionate sense of wonder is contagious. She describes herself as "a bride married to amazement" in "Poem 102: When Death Comes."

And in her poem "The Ponds," she proclaims, "Still, what I want in my life is to be willing to be dazzled—to cast aside the weight of facts and maybe even to float a little above this difficult world."

She invites us to find the magic of wonder through our willingness to be amazed.

Thinking of my enchantment with the hawk, and with the blue herons, chickadees, and the luna moth at other times in my life, I recognize the wondrous and open qualities of my character. Thankfully, mercifully, I've been "willing to be dazzled" in my darkest of times.

I believe survivors of trauma and loss can claim their willingness to be awestruck by something unexpectedly beautiful and amazing—a little act of kindness by a stranger, a golden burst of sunlight on fallen snow, a magnificent silver moon.

Are we "willing to be dazzled?"

Paths to Resilience

After my awe moment with the hawk, I savored a beautiful thought: *Our awe experiences make us resilient.*

The wonder, peace, and balance we feel are a source of strength and well-being. Surely, something in my soul must have known this back in my early twenties when I followed blue herons to their watery sanctuaries. Even though most people at that time did not recognize or understand the resilience I found through my sense of wonder, I am deeply grateful that I listened to that inner wisdom through my love of the herons.

Reflecting on the stories of Carol, Robyn, Luke, and Ricky shows us that we share common pathways to resilience through awe and wonder. Five pathways stand out as remarkably fundamental to our healing. I will celebrate and summarize these in the next section.

Pathway 1: Grounding, Mindfulness, Equanimity

I slowed down. My thoughts slowed down. I felt present in my body and not up in my head. I felt grounded, centered. I could focus.

We feel balanced and steady, able to pace ourselves, and not rushed or forcing ourselves to forge ahead. This sense of balance, ease, and grounding is fundamental for trauma survivors for regulating emotions and being able to focus. We feel solid and back in our bodies, rather than scattered or dissociated.

For example, when Luke watched his brother come out of his coma in a miraculous moment, he became quiet and attuned to him, listening and watching attentively. This crucial moment of stillness allowed Luke to regain a sense of composure and groundedness.

When Robyn was entranced by the dragonfly that unexpectedly appeared at her son's gravesite, she sat down and rested, allowing the dragonfly to land on her hand. Time seemed to stop, mercifully providing Robyn a break from her mental torment.

I remember a friend's childhood recollection of finding awe at a distressing time during the Christmas holidays. At age six, she had been rushed to her uncle's house after dark while her parents were in the hospital following a car accident. Frightened and confused, she cried and couldn't eat dinner or even a chocolate chip cookie, despite her uncle's comforting gestures. She wandered into the living room and discovered a Christmas tree decorated in glorious blue and white lights. This magical sight took her breath away, and she sat on the floor for an hour to gaze upon the tree in utter amazement. Eventually, she fell asleep. Two hours later, her parents returned from the hospital, safe and sound.

It's amazing how much we can center and balance ourselves in just one minute of awe. It is a pause that makes a world of difference for ourselves and for one another.

Pathway 2: Acceptance, Peace of Mind, Serenity

I can live with uncertainty. Life is a mystery. I don't have to have all the answers.

A reassuring way that awe builds resilience is when moments of wonder allow us to find a sense of peace and acceptance for the things we cannot "get over." Experiences of awe can provide sacred ground for people to feel safe and serene, such as the October afternoon when my father and I walked at Wolfe's Neck Woods. On that life-changing walk, we felt a sense of acceptance and peace with each other through our mutual awe of birds. Generations of collective family trauma had a fresh chance for healing in that moment of awe. Our sense of wonder was our source of peace—a safe place within ourselves as well as with each other.

This peace that comes to us through the awe of the wilderness reminds me of a poem by Wendell Berry, "The Peace of Wild Things." "For a time, I rest in the grace of the world, and I am free."

We can also feel this sense of peace through saying a prayer (such as the Serenity Prayer by Reinhold Niebuhr), or an affirmation, or lighting a candle. We can proactively set our intentions and say blessings for peace and acceptance through a ceremony or ritual.

Sometimes just a few minutes of silence opens us to a moment of wonder.

Survivors of trauma and loss can find great relief and peace in simply knowing something beautiful can take their breath away—at least for a little while. More deeply, it is reassuring to trust in the breakthroughs of peace and acceptance that come through awe, even though we live with troubling memories and heartache. Perhaps we cannot make our serenity last for long, but in moments of wonder, we can enjoy little pockets of peace.

Pathway 3: Meaning and Hope

I can live with loss that has no closure. Life is still meaningful despite the loss and suffering. I can go on. I have the will to live.

Our shared experiences of awe with other survivors help us live with purpose, meaning, and hope, despite unresolved losses and pain. When Robyn facilitates healing groups for survivors of grief and loss, she creates rituals for awe and wonder such as lighting candles, singing, or saying the names out loud of deceased loved ones. These moments of awe create a sense of beauty, honor, and meaning that help her groups face the ambiguity, pain, and lack of closure they feel with their grief. These shared experiences with other survivors help them live with unresolved loss.

Pauline Boss, who coined the term "ambiguous loss," writes about living with loss that has no closure. In her book, *The Myth of Closure: Ambiguous Loss in a Time of Pandemic and Change*, she recommends that instead of searching for closure, we open ourselves to experiences that bring meaning and hope, and that often occur when we least expect them.[4]

Awe gives us opportunities for meaning and renewed hope, especially for living with mystery, uncertainty, and situations that are messy and unpredictable. Like most everyone I know, I am becoming more and more accustomed to living with constant uncertainty and unrest in a post-pandemic, cynical, chaotically changing world (especially since the US election in 2024). Trauma and loss survivors can create opportunities for awe and wonder that help mitigate the effects of so much tension around us.

Pathway 4: New Perspectives, Openness, "Beginner's Mind"

> *Wow, I've never seen that before! That blew my mind. I had no idea. I never thought of it that way. There's a much wider world out there. I want to learn more.*

When we have experienced something that makes us wonder, our curiosity and willingness to learn are sparked. Wonder entices us, dazzles us, calls us out of our comfort zones to stretch into new concepts. We experiment with it, explore it, consider it, "try it on for size," and imagine what that concept feels like. "Wow, I wonder what that would be like."

Because awe is a self-transcending emotion that opens our minds to new perspectives, I find many similarities with the Zen Buddhist concept of beginner's mind, known as shoshin. Shunryu Suzuki brought this approach to the world with his seminal book, *Zen Mind, Beginner's Mind*. The attributes of humility, openness, unpretentiousness, and being unassuming are aspects of beginner's mind that echo how we feel in an awe experience. Beginner's mind means having a fresh pair of eyes to see the world as if for the very first time. This is often how awe feels to experiencers.

As trauma survivors, it is healthy to have a sense of beginner's mind to unlock ourselves from rigid ways of thinking and acting. Thanks to an experience of awe that opens our minds, such as when Carol unexpectedly heard her song on the radio, we can switch out of an old habit and try something new. We are ready to see what happens if we do things a different way. We are curious to find out what will happen next. And, best of all, our wonder makes us hopeful for the future.

Pathway 5: Connection, Being Part of Something Greater

There is so much more that connects us. I was alone, but I didn't feel lonely. I felt that I belonged to something much greater. It's not all about me.

In our loneliest of times, many of us have had awe-inspiring encounters with wild birds, trees, starlit skies, or oceans—and suddenly we realized we didn't feel so lonely after all. We belonged to something greater and wider, the "more-than-human" world, as David Abram, ecologist and philosopher, writes about in *The Spell of the Sensuous*. In our state of awe, we can see beyond our own human concerns and dramas, opening ourselves to a vast sense of interconnection and oneness with life around us.

Ironically, when we are alone and enjoying our wondrous times with wildlife or spiritual practices, we can restore ourselves as relational beings and remember how we naturally reach for connection, even with the sky. We feel energized, hopeful, and smaller in a good way, knowing that we still belong in the world where we can hold space with others in all life forms.

And if we were to share a moment of awe with someone else or with a like-minded group of people, we might invite more engagement with ease, spontaneity, or open-mindedness. We feel curious and wondrous, being willing to listen and to be enthralled, tuning in to others in our company.

Consider what millions of Americans in the path of totality during the April 2024 solar eclipse exclaimed as the sky darkened: "Oh, wow—have you ever seen anything like this?" Our awe generated deep emotions, chills of excitement, goosebumps, tears of joy, and a sense of oneness with others. This amazing moment was shared with others on top of mountains, in open fields, in city parks, and on ocean beaches. Many of us could vicariously enjoy the path of totality that other viewers were experiencing through social media.

These wondrous encounters take on a whole new meaning when they are shared—whether with a friend or with multitudes of people. Awe shifts our energy and focus outward. Researcher Michelle Shiota attests, "When I am less focused on myself, on my own goals and needs and thoughts in my head, I have more bandwidth to notice you and what you may be experiencing."[5] Echoing her words, considering how we have "more bandwidth to notice," awe gives us a more unbiased, open-minded way of seeing the people around us. The humbling moments that take our breath away allow us to see each other in a whole new light. We are likely to be less selfish and more compassionate during an awe experience. People watching an eclipse, or an aurora borealis, or a brilliant Olympic gymnast, or a Taylor

Swift concert are more likely to feel a sense of unity, belonging, and connection rather than self-centeredness.

Awe brings out the best of our prosocial behaviors.

Creating Community Through Awe and Wonder

When we have an experience of awe, we often want to share it, even months or years later. We might share this moment in stories, in person, in writing, through video, or song. People are hungry to express the moments that took their breath away.

My friends love to share their awe and wonder stories. One local friend, Noreen, called me, excitedly announcing, "I saw a cardinal today!" She believes in the healing power of signs and synchronicities, and that her mother is in touch with her through cardinal visitations, giving her faith that "Mom is checking in on me," as she describes it.

Another friend, Sarah, sent me a greeting card with a blue heron drawing. Inside the card was an invitation to visit her in Maine for New Year's Eve. She wrote about a "miracle" that her nephew was finally in rehab and getting the treatment he needed.

Another friend, Rob, called to tenderly share his story about a recent dream where his deceased daughter visited him. "She came to me just before Christmas. What a gift!"

Awe and wonder experiences beckon us to share our life-affirming, amazing bursts of hope with others. I am glad I can foster those stories with my friends, building deeper, soulful connections.

Even though I have a few dear friends, and though I deeply enjoy moments of awe and wonder, I still battle inner demons and outer destructive forces. I could easily fall into cynicism, bitterness, and loneliness. Most of my peers have comfortably retired, and most of them have grandchildren (appearing in photos lovingly posted on Instagram and Facebook)—and fly off to London or California, though I can hardly afford to drive two hours up to Maine to visit a friend. I have no kids, no grandkids, and no spouse, but I post photos of my projects and my books—my beloved creations.

And it is ridiculously, needlessly cruel to compare myself to others. I refuse to "go there" with a long list of contrasts. Instead, I proclaim that I love writing. I cherish my sense of wonder. I'm just fine with a cup of French roast coffee, sitting by a window, gazing at swirling ribbons of snow in a wintry morning breeze. And I'm utterly grateful that I still have my faculties for watching, listening, and marveling.

There is much, *much* more to celebrate in my life that I have co-created with the good, local people I've met.

I have built a community, and come hell or high water, no matter what happens in the world, I have a group of people who share a common purpose. Amazingly, we are all connected through our love of awe and wonder. Through my volunteer work with Robyn Houston-Bean and her grief support organization, the Sun Will Rise Foundation, late in 2023, we launched our Healing Through Wonder Project, and now we enjoy a growing network of enthusiastic peers.

Through my involvement with the Healing Through Wonder Project, I collaborate with many recovery and peer support organizations throughout Massachusetts such as Peer Support Community Partners, and I blog for the Health Story Collaborative to share our stories. Our project has been a magnet for healthcare providers, social workers, educators, and chaplains, as well as individuals and families who join in storytelling groups.

I'm in awe of how people come together to create safe, compassionate places for recovering from trauma, loss, and addiction. In caring and thoughtful support groups, I have seen how shared experiences of awe can be a source of community as well as of resilience. We learn from our stories, and we record them on YouTube and other social media. We find meaning and wisdom when we listen to our stories at later times.

As my hawk experience and my heron encounters have taught me, awe and wonder moments lift us out of our headspace, out of our isolation and loneliness, and out of our rush to judgment. And when we share our awe-inspiring stories, the healing of that awe experience is even more meaningful.

Decades ago, back in the days of following the blue herons to my river sanctuaries in Maine and Virginia, I had no idea that I would end up sharing my stories with the world. I never dreamed that other trauma and loss survivors would be so willing and open to share their experiences of awe and wonder.

And it astounds me even more how our moments of wonder, *and* our sense of wonder, have given us the resilience, not only to survive, but to love our lives. Despite the broken and wounded parts of ourselves that never seem to fit with the good stuff in us, somehow, thanks to unexpected bursts of wonder, the light shines through those cracks in ourselves. We don't even have to put forth lots of effort for that awe-inspiring moment to light us up. It just happens naturally. Something naturally takes our breath away—the rising silver moon, or our cat scampering into our office. We are suddenly transformed—and we didn't even do anything to "deserve" it. It just happens when a blue heron lands ten feet away, or when a song pops on the radio.

I won't split hairs or fret trying to verify if the spirit of my grandmother or my father is truly communicating through my wonder of chickadees or hawks. I'm fine, just saying "maybe."

I won't ignore the blue heron soaring over me when I stand shivering at the gas station pumping my car in the cold rain. I'll look up with reverence, and my day will change for the better.

And I won't discount my little joys of synchronicities and signs, despite the elegant, brilliant logic that would explain these coincidences as random events. I would rather give myself something intriguing to wonder about—because wonder restores me. Why can't the neuroscience of wonder, the biology of birds, and the ecstasy of spirituality all coexist quite marvelously in my mind—each category a treasure trove of discovery? Any of these paths, through science, art, or spirituality, is wondrous. Why tamper with these?

My wonder comes to me tamper-proof, natural, unadulterated. When I least expect it, wonder arrives as a gift with no strings attached. I'll take it, even if the cynics of the world pity me. I'll take it and be fulfilled—and grateful.

I'll take it—even when I don't have a clue what the heck is going on. It happens for some amazing reason I might never understand.

It happens and will keep happening—and that is all I need to live well.

Today, by the way, one of my oldest, best friends, Jill, called me. She excitedly announced, "I saw a blue heron this morning, and I thought this was a sign to call you!"

Naturally, joyously, as she sipped her peppermint tea, we reminisced about chickadees, herons, hawks, dreams, and rivers.

Notes

1. Dacher Keltner, *Awe: The New Science of Everyday Wonder and How It Can Transform Your Life* (New York: Penguin Books, 2023), xx.
2. Paul Wright, MD, "The neuroscience and health benefits of experiencing awe and wonder," *Nuvance Health* (August 9, 2024).
3. Maria Shriver, "Maria Shriver interviews the famously private poet Mary Oliver," *Oprah Magazine* (2011).
4. Pauline Boss, *The Myth of Closure: Ambiguous Loss in a Time of Pandemic and Change* (New York: W.W. Norton and Company, 2021).
5. David Robson, "Awe: The little earthquake that could free your mind," *BBC* (January 6, 2022).

Appendix
A Friendly Guide to Wondrous Things

Movies, Books, Music, and Videos for Wonder Seekers and Wonder Makers

Welcome to my guide to wondrous creations and media that I've curated and annotated with joy and gratitude!

My guide is a celebration and "show-and-tell" of wondrous things that I've thoughtfully selected from my experience as an educator, rehabilitation counselor, group facilitator, and expressive arts specialist. (I hold a Bachelor of Fine Arts degree in theater and dance, and a Master of Science degree in rehabilitation counseling.)

Ever since the age of nineteen when I first began teaching dance and drama to children with disabilities, I've tapped into and applied the wonders of poetry, music, theater, team-building games, person-centered and expressive arts therapies, recreation therapies, wordplay and storytelling activities, crafts, and more. I've applied these activities with teens in substance use prevention programs, seniors with dementia, bereavement support groups, hospice volunteer training, support groups for cancer survivors, traumatic brain injury support groups, support groups for anxiety disorders, and others.

For over four decades, I've witnessed that even two minutes of sharing a wonder-enhancing activity in a group is well worth the effort. Those minutes can make all the difference in bringing people together as a group and into the present moment. Whether we are watching planets through the Webb telescope on screen, or listening to the soundtrack of *Interstellar*, or reading out loud a poem by Mary Oliver, we can infuse a fresh burst of wonder into our day.

In my first book, *The Art of Comforting: What to Say and Do for People in Distress*, I provided a comprehensive list of resources called "A Little Guidebook to Comforting Things," in which I lovingly included comforting things that were popular with my groups. Now, for my guide to wondrous things, I've updated and added to those previous lists—*and I've had a blast putting it all together!*

Educators, group facilitators, activities and recreation specialists, psychotherapists, or *anyone* who wants to explore new ways to find wonder will hopefully discover (or rediscover) resources to spark their curiosity. This is certainly not an exhaustive or complete list. Hopefully these resources can serve as a kind of icebreaker for activating ourselves as wonder seekers, wonder chasers, and wonder makers.

Section 1: Activity Guides to Inspire Wonder

Guidebooks to Inspire Activities That Enhance Our Sense of Wonder

- *Wonder Seeker: 52 Ways to Wake Up Your Creativity and Find Your Joy* by Andrea Scher (Harper Design, 2021). Wow—for all ages! The activities presented in this lively, colorful, and delightfully accessible book offer ideas and inspiration for anyone who wants to bring wonder into their day.

- *Exploring Nature Activity Book for Kids: 50 Creative Projects to Spark Curiosity in the Outdoors (Exploring for Kids Activity Books and Journals)* by Kim Andrews (Callisto Kids, 2019). Generously full of actionable, realistic activities to enjoy with young children (ages 6–12).

- *A Place for Wonder: Reading and Writing Nonfiction in the Primary Grades* by Georgia Heard and Jennifer McDonough (Routledge, 2009). This guide sparks curiosity and enhances a sense of wonder that lasts a lifetime.

Websites to Inspire Wonder Activities and Expand Our Curiosity

- **The Greater Good in Education "Module 8.5 Awe for Students"** provides a comprehensive curriculum for educators (lower elementary through high school). https://ggie.berkeley.edu/practice/module-8-5/

- **TED Ed:** Create and curate your own lessons for yourself, or as a parent, or an educator. Enormously vast worlds to explore that can be accessed through this imaginative and exploratory site. https://ed.ted.com

- **Mental Floss:** A fascinating website full of amazing facts that make us wonder out loud. We can spark our sense of discovery and wonder just by visiting this website and learning something new and amazing every day. www.mentalfloss.com

Section 2: Awe-Inspiring People

Conversations with Awe-Inspiring People

- **Simone Biles** Video: Good Morning America, "Simone Biles opens up about mental health battle"
- **Andrew Garfield** Video: "I hope this grief stays with me." Andrew Garfield talks with Stephen Colbert about living with grief after the death of his mother.
- **Brandon Stratton** Video: CBS Mornings, "Street photographer documents *Humans of New York*" (Brandon Stratton)

Documentaries and Biopics About Awe-Inspiring People

- *An Angel at My Table* (Janet Frame)
- *A Beautiful Day in the Neighborhood* (Fred Rogers)
- *Erin Brockovich*
- *Ghandi* (Mahatma Ghandi)
- *Hidden Figures* (Katherine Johnson, Dorothy Vaughan, and Mary Jackson)
- *The King's Speech* (King George VI)
- *Lion* (Saroo Brierley)
- *My Left Foot* (Christy Brown)
- *The Miracle Worker* (Helen Keller and Anne Sullivan)
- *Nyad* (Diana Nyad)

- *Ray* (Ray Charles)
- *Rocketman* (Elton John)
- *Stronger* (Jeff Bauman)
- *Seabiscuit* (Jockey "Red" Pollard)
- *The Theory of Everything* (Stephen Hawking)
- *Tina* (Tina Turner)
- *Walk the Line* (Johnny Cash)

Books About Awe-Inspiring People

- *The Doctors Blackwell: How Two Pioneering Sisters Brought Medicine to Women and Women to Medicine* by Janice P. Nimura
- *Humans of New York* by Brandon Stratton

Memoirs About Facing Adversity, Disability, or Mental Illness

- *Angela's Ashes* by Frank McCourt
- *The Center Does Not Hold: My Journey Through Madness* by Elyn Saks
- *Diary of a Young Girl* by Anne Frank
- *I Know Why the Caged Bird Sings* by Maya Angelou
- *My Left Foot* by Christy Brown
- *The Noonday Demon: An Atlas of Depression* by Andrew Solomon
- *The Story of My Life* by Helen Keller

Memoirs About Facing Grief and Loss

- *Here If You Need Me: A True Story* by Kate Braestrup
- *The Long Goodbye: A Memoir* by Meghan O'Rourke
- *Grief Is Love: Living with Loss* by Marisa Renee Lee
- *Grief is a Sneaky Bitch: An Uncensored Guide to Navigating Loss* by Lisa Keefauver

Memoirs About Facing Trauma or Complex Trauma

- *Complex PTSD: From Surviving to Thriving* by Pete Walker
- *To Be Loved: A Story of Truth, Trauma, and Transformation* by Frank Anderson
- *What My Bones Know: A Memoir of Healing from Complex Trauma by* Stephanie Foo
- *Stolen Childhoods: Thriving After Abuse* by Shari Botwin

Section 3: Sharing Awe in Groups of People

Videos of Amazing Crowd Vibes in Action

- America's Got Talent with the Mayyas and more: "3 Groups That Will Leave Your Jaw on the FLOOR! | AGT 2022"
- Coldplay, "Fix You" (Glastonbury 2024); Chris Martin is singing with Michael J. Fox.

- "England fans singing 'Sweet Caroline' before the Euro 2020 Final 11/07/21"
- "Red Sox Fans Singing 'Sweet Caroline' During 2018 World Series | Boston, MA |October 23, 2018"
- Flashmob: "Flashmob—Stairway to Heaven"
- Flashmob: "Wish You Were Here—Flashmob—Pink Floyd Project Tour 2024 (The Netherlands)"
- "AMAZING—Flash Mob—Started by one little girl—Ode to Joy"
- "110,000 FANS SINGING 'MR. BRIGHTSIDE'"
- "Thriller Dance—Michael Jackson—New York City Halloween Parade 2024"

Section 4: Nature

Websites to Inspire Wonder in Nature

- Paths of Learning: Nature-Based Learning: pathsoflearning.net
- Roots and Shoots (The Jane Goodall Institute): rootsandshoots.org
- James Webb Space Telescope: webbtelescope.org

Books to Inspire Wonder in the Natural World

- *The Comfort of Crows: A Backyard Year* by Margaret Renkl

- *The Hidden Life of Trees: What They Feel, How They Communicate—Discoveries from a Secret World* by Peter Wohlleben
- *An Immense World: How Animal Senses Reveal the Hidden Realms Around Us* by Ed Yong
- *Providence of a Sparrow: Lessons from a Life Gone to the Birds* by Chris Chester
- *Refuge: An Unnatural History of Family and Place* by Terry Tempest Williams
- *The Sense of Wonder: A Celebration of Nature for Parents and Children* by Rachel Carson
- *Sisters of the Earth: Women's Prose and Poetry About Nature* edited by Lorraine Anderson
- *Something in the Woods Loves You* by Jarod K. Anderson
- *The Spell of the Sensuous: Perception and Language in a More-Than-Human World* by David Abram
- *The Wonder of Birds: What They Tell Us About Ourselves, the World, and a Better Future* by Jim Robbins
- *World of Wonders: In Praise of Fireflies, Whale Sharks, and Other Astonishments* by Aimee Nezhukumatathil and Fumi Nakamura
- *The Universe in Verse: 15 Portals to Wonder Through Science & Poetry* by Maria Popova (Author), Ofra Amit (Illustrator)

Nature Videos and Documentaries

- *The Beauty of Earth* ("The Beauty of" Channel)
- "Diane Arkenstone—Elements of Nature (Official Music Video)"
- *Forests*, a film by Louie Schwartzberg (excerpt 1)
- *Hidden Miracles of the Natural World* (Louie Schwartzberg)
- *The Octopus Teacher* (Documentary)
- *One Day on Earth* (Part 4 of 4)
- "The Secret Language of Trees" (Real Science Series)
- *Winged Migration* (Documentary)
- *Yosemite HDII*

Section 5: Awe-Inspiring Music

Videos on YouTube

The following are particularly stunning music *and* imagery videos—amazing feats of cinematography, art, and music beautifully coordinated.

- "The Cinematic Orchestra—Arrival of the Birds"
- *Baraka* (1992)—"Finale" HD (Soundtrack by Michael Stearns)
- Coldplay, "Coldplay—Moon Music (A Film for the Future)"

- Coldplay, "Coldplay—ONE WORLD (A Film for the Future)"
- Coldplay, "Coldplay—A Skyful of Stars (Live at River Plate)"
- Hent Telenn Breizh, "THE GAEL from *The Last of the Mohicans*—Breizh Pan Celtic"
- *Interstellar* Main theme music—With deep space video—Hans Zimmer
- Jon Hopkins, "Jon Hopkins—Ritual (Palace) (Official Video)"
- "Thousand-Hand Guan Yin (Samsara)"

More Awe-Inspiring Music

- America, "A Horse with No Name"
- Jon Anderson and Tangerine Dream, "Loved by the Sun" from the *Legend* soundtrack
- Louis Armstrong, "What a Wonderful World"
- Stephen J. Anderson, "Most Epic Music of All Time—African Skies"
- Beach House, "Superstar"
- Blue Wave Studio, "Counting Galaxies"
- Sarah Brightman, *In Paradisum*
- Celtic Woman, "The Voice"
- Enya, "Aniron" (Extended HD), "Only Time"
- Aretha Franklin, "Spirit in the Dark"

APPENDIX

- Gustav Holst, "Neptune" (from *The Planets*, a classic far ahead of its time from 1917)
- HAEVN feat. Neco Novellas—*Great Mother* (Official Music Video)
- Loreena McKennitt, "The Mystic's Dream"
- Jean Michel Jarre, *Oxygene II* (remastered from a gorgeous, trippy 1976 classic)
- Moody Blues, "Your Wildest Dreams" or "Tuesday Afternoon"
- Joanne Shenandoah, "Peace and Power" or "Mother of Nations"
- Paul Simon and Art Garfunkel, "Scarborough Fair" Remastered Study (HQ Audio)
- *Sleeping Beauty* (Disney), "I Wonder" song
- Taylor Swift, "Snow on the Beach" (Lyric Video) feat. Lana Del Rey
- Riverdance, "Cloudsong" (Riverdance 2010)
- Vangelis, "Antarctic Echoes," from the *Antarctica* soundtrack
- Eric Whitacre, *Deep Field: Earth Choir*
- Ralph Vaughan Williams, *Fantasia on a Theme by Thomas Tallis*

Section 6: Visual Awe

Awe-Inspiring Visual Experiences Through Film

- *Amelie*
- *Arrival*
- *Avatar* (2009)
- *Bladerunner* (1982)
- *Bladerunner 2049*
- *The Boy and the Heron*
- *Chronos*
- *Close Encounters of the Third Kind*
- *The Grand Budapest Hotel*
- *Gravity*
- *Interstellar*
- *Lawrence of Arabia*
- *Life of Pi*
- *Lord of the Rings: Fellowship of the Ring*
- *Spirited Away*
- *The Tree of Life*
- *Wicked*
- *Winged Migration*
- *2001: A Space Odyssey*

Virtual Museum Tours (Immersive Learning Experiences)

- Smithsonian National Museum of Natural History
- The British Museum
- The Louvre
- The Metropolitan Museum of Art (Met 360 Project)
- MoMA (Museum of Modern Art in NYC)
- Chicago Institute of Art

Section 7: Spirituality and Religion

Admittedly, it's a delicate task to select media to fit such a vast, varied, and highly charged subject. But from my professional experience (e.g., leading activities for groups of elderly adults of different faiths at an assisted living community), I've witnessed that most people enjoy the topic of gratitude and blessings as well as listening to sublime, sacred music. We are *exploring and wondering*, not necessarily subscribing to what we experience. Being able to see through different lenses can open us to wonder.

Websites to Explore Wonder Through Spirituality and Religion

These websites provide ideas for spiritual practices to spark our wonder.

- Beliefnet: Beliefnet.com
- Grateful Living: Gratefulness.org
- Spirituality & Health: Spiritualityhealth.com

Videos to Enhance Wonder About Spirituality and Religion

- *Baraka*: "A Journey Through Faith" (World Religions OST)
- "Charlotte Church—Pie Jesu (Live from Brixton Academy)"
- Bill Douglas, "Deep Peace" Music Video
- "The five major world religions—John Bellaimey" (TED-Ed)
- "A Grateful Day with Brother David Steindl-Rast—Gratefulness.org"
- "Hildegard of Bingen: O Fire of The Holy Spirit, Comforter | O ignis Spiritus"

Books to Enhance Wonder Through Spirituality and Religion

- *Anam Cara* by John O'Donohue
- *The Awakened Brain: The New Science of Spirituality and Our Quest for an Inspired Life* by Lisa Miller, PhD
- *Blessings: Prayers and Declarations for a Heartful Life* by Julia Cameron
- *Care of the Soul* by Thomas Moore
- *Chicken Soup for the Soul: Angels and Miracles* by Amy Newmark
- *A Cup of Comfort for Inspiration: Uplifting Stories That Will Brighten Your Day* by Colleen Sell

- *Enduring Grace: Living Portraits of Seven Women Mystics* by Carol Flinders
- *Mystics and Miracles: True Stories of Lives Touched by God* by Bert Ghezzi
- *One River, Many Wells: Wisdom Springing from Global Faiths* by Matthew Fox
- *Ordinary Mysticism: Your Life as Sacred Ground* by Mirabai Starr
- *A Pocketful of Miracles: Prayers, Meditations, and Affirmations to Nurture Your Spirit Every Day of the Year* by Joan Borysenko, PhD
- *The Power of Myth* by Joseph Campbell
- *The Power of Now: A Guide to Spiritual Enlightenment* by Eckhardt Tolle
- *Signs: The Secret Language of the Universe* by Laura Lynn Jackson
- *The Signs: The New Science of How to Trust Your Instincts* by Dr. Tara Swart, MD, PhD
- *The Tao of Psychology: Synchronicity and the Self* by Jean Shinoda Bolen
- *To Bless the Space Between Us* by John O'Donohue
- *Women in Praise of the Sacred: 43 Centuries of Spiritual Poetry by Women* edited by Jane Hirshfield (This book includes poems from a variety of religions.)

Section 8: Birth and Death

Websites

- Mom in the Six: "Thirty Birth Photos That Show Pure, Beautiful Love" by Jill Saunders: mominthesix.com
- Dr. Christopher Kerr (Hospice & Palliative Care, Buffalo): End-of-Life Experience Research: drchristopherkerr.com
- End Well Project: A nonprofit dedicated to quality of life at the end of life, and researching end-of-life experiences: endwellproject.org
- IANDS (International Association for Near-Death Studies), Inc: iands.org

Books on Wonders of End-of-Life Experiences

- *Death is But a Dream: Finding Hope and Meaning at Life's End* by Christopher Kerr, MD, PhD, and Carine Mardorossian, PhD
- *When We Die: Extraordinary Experiences at Life's End* by Kenneth Doka, PhD

Section 9: Epiphany

Books on Wonders of Epiphanies

- *Chicken Soup for the Soul: The Best Advice I Ever Heard: 101 Stories of Epiphanies and Wise Words* by Amy Newmark

- *Epiphany: True Stories of Sudden Insight to Inspire, Encourage and Transform, Expanded Edition* by Elise Ballard

YouTube Clips of Epiphanies

- "G.W. Bailey Talks with Elise Ballard about Epiphanies & His Story"
- *The Miracle Worker*, "9/10 Movie Clip—She Knows! (1962) HD"
- *Soul*, "Epiphany" (Clip)

Section 10: Poetry

Poetry can open us to wonderment through words that instantly transport us to other places and times. I have created a list of poems that can evoke a sense of wonder with groups of people, particularly when read out loud.

- **Maya Angelou**

    "Amazement Awaits"
    "A Brave and Startling Truth"

- **Wendell Berry**

    "Grace"
    "The Peace of Wild Things"
    "What We Need Is Here"
    "Woods"

- **William Blake**

  "Eternity"
  "Spring"
  "The Tyger"

- **Robert Bly**

  "Dusk in the Country"
  "Living at the End of Time"

- **Billy Collins**

  "Today"

- **E.E. Cummings**

  "I Carry Your Heart With Me"

- **Emily Dickinson**

  "Hope Is the Thing with Feathers"
  "I Have a Bird in Spring"
  "To March" ("Dear March—Come in")

- **Ralph Waldo Emerson**

  "To Laugh Often and Much"

- **Joy Harjo**

  "Ah, Ah"
  "Eagle Poem"
  "Remember"

- **Langston Hughes**

  "In Time of Silver Rain"
  "The Power of a Circle"

- **Pablo Neruda**

    "Bird"

    "Songs of Togetherness"

- **Mary Oliver**

    "Heron Rises from the Dark, Summer Pond"

    "Poem 102: When Death Comes"

    "Poem of the One World"

    "The Ponds"

    "Wild Geese"

- **Jalal al-Din Rumi**

    "Come, Come Whoever You Are"

    "Don't Go Back to Sleep"

- **Edna St. Vincent Millay**

    "Afternoon on a Hill"

- **Walt Whitman**

    "Song at Sunset"

    "Song of the Open Road"

    "When I Heard the Learn'd Astronomer"

- **William Wordsworth**

    "My Heart Leaps Up"

    "I Wandered Lonely as a Cloud"

    "Written in March"

- **William Butler Yeats**

    "The Lake Isle of Innisfree"

Section 11: Books About Awe and Wonder

Introductions to the Neuroscience of Awe and Wonder

- *Awe: The New Science of Everyday Wonder and How It Can Transform Your Life* by Dacher Keltner
- *The Power of Wonder: The Extraordinary Emotion That Will Change the Way You Live, Learn, and Lead* by Monica C. Parker

Personal and Philosophical Reflections on Awe and Wonder

- *The Enchanted Life: Reclaiming the Magic and Wisdom of the Natural World* by Sharon Blackie
- *Enchantment: Awakening Wonder in an Anxious Age* by Katherine May
- *In Awe: Rediscover Your Childlike Wonder to Unleash Inspiration, Meaning, and Joy* by John O'Leary

ACKNOWLEDGMENTS

I'm in awe of the four courageously honest people who were profiled in this book—and who stood by this project for the long haul. More than awestruck, I'm grateful and humbled by their generosity to tell their stories in such fine, glorious detail even when a narrative was fraught with grief, terror, or illness.

As survivors of trauma and loss sharing breathtaking moments of wonder, they attested, through intricate details, how their awe-filled encounters made them resilient. More than spotting silver linings, or seeing through rose-colored lenses, or forcing positivity, their profound moments of awe not only transformed their lives but may have saved their lives.

Speaking of details in their stories, when we say, "the devil is in the details," these storytellers showed me that—more often than not—*angels* are in those details! Indeed, their stories of awe and wonder are celebrations of the many splendid details that we observe when pausing in a wondrous moment. In these instances when time seems to stand still, we can truly see the magic and providence of the fine, delicate details that make our lives wondrous.

Given their generous act of storytelling in such vivid detail, I heartily thank the four people who opened their lives to share their stories for *Healing Through Wonder*: Robyn Houston-Bean, Luke Schmaltz, Carol Bowers, and Ricky Allen. I hope readers have felt the warmth and spirit of these brave, wise people through their radiant stories of not only surviving, but of living life to the fullest through their sense of wonder.

Offering support, encouragement, and recommending a storyteller to be profiled, I would like to thank Annie Brewster, MD, founder of the Health Story Collaborative. Dr. Brewster has also featured and promoted my blog posts for the "Healing Through Wonder Project" on her organization's website.

I would also like to thank those who participated in my "Healing Through Wonder Storytelling Project" on YouTube with guests through the Sun Will Rise Foundation, founded by Robin Houston-Bean, and SADOD (Support After a Death by Overdose). In addition to Luke, Carol, and Robyn, the participating storytellers on this channel included Tanya Lord, Gary Carter, Don Lipstein, Mary Peckham, Tavyn Bryn Thuringer, Olivia Wagner, and Irina Veron. Guests from other organizations included Rev. Dr. Lori Whittemore, Director of the Spiritual Care Services of Maine, and Dave Roberts, Professor of Psychology at Utica University and Host of the Teaching Journeys Podcast.

I would love to thank Amy Handy for her independent editing services and warm reassurance in the development and refinement of my manuscript.

I joyously thank Jacqueline Flynn, Senior Acquisitions Editor at Bloomsbury Publishing, and her editorial assistant, Mikayla Lindsay, for believing in my project from the get-go and bringing it through the entire process of publication. Thanks to their effort and guidance, I'm profoundly honored to have joined the wide, amazing network of authors with Bloomsbury Publishing. I would also like to thank

David Bailey at Bloomsbury for his generosity and care during the production phase of this book.

I'm blessed to have had the solid support of my agent at FinePrint Literary Management, Peter Rubie, who believed that my book had "a lot of promise" back in early 2024 when I first shared my proposal with him. I'm deeply grateful for the connection that opened the opportunity to become a Bloomsbury author.

Finally, I'm grateful to my friends and colleagues who have valued my pursuits, adventures, misadventures, and sacrifices as a writer. They've listened to my ideas, insights, and imaginings long before these thoughts turned into books. I've treasured our times together as they shared their wonder, joy, lovingly honest feedback, and amazing sense of humor.

INDEX

Abenaki Native tribe   58
ability to listen   138
Abram, David   204
acceptance   25, 62, 201–2
accommodation, need for   76
ACE (Adverse Childhood Experiences)   33
affirmations   179, 201–2
Allen, Ricky   145–57
ambiguous loss   202–3
American Psychological Association   70, 104
Andrews, Ted   69
Angelou, Maya   189
anticipatory thinking   73
anxiety   121, 137, 151, 154, 163, 167–8
appreciation and reverence   181
Archimedes   187
astrologer   17–18
attention   165
attunement   42–3
autonomy   121
awareness   71–2
awe   67, *see also* wonder
   activities to cultivate everyday   188–9
   care for others, inspires us to   153–6
   definitions   71–2
   -enhancing favorites   188
   in groups of people   169–71, 216–17
   healing through sharing, and wonder   127–42
   -inspiring acts of people   167–70, 214–16
   -inspiring art and artists   174–5
   -inspiring music   173–5, 219–21
   -inspiring visual experiences   176, 222–3
   and living with uncertainty   104
   moments, frequency of   78
   physical sensations of   75–6
   and prosocial behavior   72–3, 155–6
   sharing, in relationships and groups   95–9
   source of   4–5
   underappreciated emotions of   70
   unexpected moments of   79
   walk   78
   well-being and   72
   wonder and   69, 97
Awe Experience Scale   74–5

back to my senses   24–7
balance   2
beginner's mind and resilience   203–4
beholding   42–3, 181–2
being open   100, *see also* healing
being part of something greater, resilience   204–6
belief
   systems   101–2
   worship and   177
Belle Isle at James River Park, Virginia   24

INDEX

belonging   4–5, 93, 98, 139, 198
Berry, Wendell   189
Biles, Simone   167
biographies of real-life heroes   169
birth and death   183–6, 226
birthing consciousness   183–4
Bishop, Elizabeth   8
Blake, William   40
blue heron   20–3, 58, 64, 67, 71, 75
blue notebook   43–7
Bly, Robert   56
Bolen, Jean Shinoda   181
books
   about awe and wonder   230
   of blessings   179
Boss, Pauline   105–6, 202–3
Bowers, Carol   127–42
Brewster, Annie   86
Buddhism   178
bullying   146, 153–4

Cameron, Julia   179
candle gazing   182
candlelight event   170
Caodaism   178
Carson, Rachel   2–3, 40, 68–9, 165
channeled spirit   23
chickadees   8–9, 26–7, 58–9, 64, 67
Chirico, Alice   71
Christianity   177–8
client-driven approach   51
collective effervescence   169–71
community
   creation through awe and wonder   206–10
   rituals   98
companionship   40, 112
concentration problem   192
Confucianism   178
connectedness   76

connection   123–4
   resilience and   204–6
counseling and psychotherapy   51
courage   95
Covid-19 pandemic   1, 64
Craigmillar Festival Society   50
creating community through awe   206
critical thinking   70
   skills   101
criticism   139
curiosity   141
cynicism   164

death wish   23
default mode network (DMN)   73, 154–5, 186, 197
dementia   171, 185
depression   65, 151, 154
   empty and   147
determination   2, 128, 168
devotionals   179
Devotions   198
Dickinson, Emily   40
dignity   2
   grace and   42
disenfranchised grief   139–40
Disenfranchised Grief: Recognizing Hidden Sorrow   139
dissociation   15–16, 31
distraction   124, 192–3
divine faith   8
documentaries and biopic movies   168
Doka, Kenneth   105–6, 139–40, 184
domestic violence   1, 31–5, 53
dopamine release   196
dreams   183
drug addiction   127, 129, 148

Egyptians and the Bennu   7–8, 39–40
Eight Wonders of Life (Dacher Keltner's term)   166
Einstein, Albert   187
ELEs, *see* end of life experiences (ELEs)
emotion/emotional   114, 146, 166, 171
  damage   112
  and rage   113
  support   112
empathic women (empaths)   34
empathy   34, 53, 104, 128
end of life experiences (ELEs)   183–4, 226
ephemeris   17
epiphany   186–8, 226–7
equanimity   200–1
Estes, Clarissa Pinkola   69
exploitation   164

failing psychotherapy   29–35
faith   2
  in humanity   122
family trauma   201
fear   121, 156, 167–8
  -mongering   164
fentanyl overdose   132
film, awe-inspiring visual experiences   176
Five-Factor Model of Personality   77, 100–1
force   25
forest bathing   172, 182
400 Friends and No One to Call   64
Fox, Matthew   182
Francis of Assisi   40
freedom   129, 135
Friendly Guide to Wondrous Things   211–30
Frost, Robert   188

Gandhi   16
Generation Z   121
"Godwink" books   181
Googins Island   58
goosebumps   75–6, 139
grace   2
  dignity and   42
gratitude   22, 58–9, 153, 178–9
Greater Good Science Center   70, 166
grief   19, 94, 104–6, 138, 202, *see also* loneliness
  isolating type of   139
grounding   49–50
  and recovery from grief   24
  and relief   25
  resilience   200–1
guardedness   124
guidance and knowledge   53
guru Satchidananda   17

habitual patterns of thinking   71–2
Haidt, Jonathan   121
Hand Delivered Hope   94
harbinger   39–41
Hari, Johann   165, 192
Harjo, Joy   56
healing   97, 105
  grief   104–6, 171, 138, 202
  through sharing awe and wonder   127–42
Healing Through Wonder Project   82, 85, 99–100, 207
Health Story Collaborative   82, 86, 153, 207
Hermes   11–12
heroin   129, *see also* drug addiction
Heron Behaviors   24, 37–43
Heron Lore   8
Hinduism   178

Hitchiti Tribe of the Muscogee-speaking people of Georgia 8
hope 107, 202–3
   inspiration and 80
hopelessness 156
Houston-Bean, Robyn 3–4, 81–2, 89–108
   dragonfly moment 92–5
   grief support organization 207
human
   self-consciousness 21
   spirit, wonders of 169
humanity 165–7
humility 153
hypervigilance 15, 31

illness and grief 151
imaginations 195
inflammation 73, 197
Ingerman, Sandra 69
injustice 164
inner guidance 52
in-person human interaction 120–1
inspiration(al)
   literature 171
   news stories 168
   speaker 170
intensive psychotherapy 168
interconnection and awe 72–3
International Association for Near Death Studies (IANDS) 185
Islam 178
isolation 123–4

Jackson, Laura Lynn 181
James, William 69
Jean Baker Miller Institute 53
Jewett, Sarah Orne 8
Joan of Arc 16
Judaism 178
Jung, Carl 69, 181

keepsakes of the soul 45
Keller, Helen 188
Keltner, Dacher 70–1, 77, 166–87, 196
Kerr, Christopher 184
kindness and caring 152
Kotschnig, Walter 100
Kross, Ethan 72

labor of love 27
language 115
   of empathy 53
learning survival skills 128
Lerner, Rokelle 179
lessons from herons 35–6
Lewis Ginter Botanical Gardens 83
life-affirming
   movie 170
   wonder 2
Life After Life 17
limits to finding awe online 102
loneliness 16, 64–5, 139–40, 163
   hopelessness and 80
Lotti, Rhonda 94

Maine 56–62
mantras 179
meaning
   awe and 72–3
   resilience 202–3
mental health 70
   care 51
   illness 152, 154
Merriam-Webster 186
Merton, Thomas 69
mindful focus 24
mindfulness 200–1
mirror gazing 182
misconceptions and realities about awe 76–80
Moody, Raymond 17

Moore, Thomas   69
moral beauty   167–8
Mother Teresa   16
museums   175–6, 223
music   173–5, 219–21
mystery   101–2

narcissistic   164
National Alliance on Mental Illness (NAMI)   145, 151–2
National Institutes of Health   70
Native Americans   8
natural world   171–3, 217–19
nature-oriented experiences   172–3
near-death experiences   13–14, 17, 185
negative self-talk   73
neuroscience   2–3
   myths and biases   76–80
   researchers of awe   69–73
New Age Spirituality   16, 20, 31, 34
new perspectives, resilience   203–4
Newton, Isaac   187
Nouwen, Henri   69

O'Donohue, John   69, 179
Oliver, Mary   5, 8, 56, 81, 188–9, 198–9
O Magazine   198
oneness   93, 139, 205
open/openness   100–1, 141
   to experience   77, 100
   humility and   94
   and imaginative minds   103
   -minded and curious   137
   resilience   203–4
   of spirit   193
optical illusions   176
overactive imagination   16
overthinking   192, 195–6
oxytocin   196

Parker, Monica   160
Parkinson's disease   174
passion for finding awe   116
patience   2, 25
   art of timing and   37–8
peace   61–2
   of mind   201–2
   serenity and   201–3
person/personal
   -centered approach   51–2
   growth   140–1
   resilience   52
   resistance   165
Phillips, Wilson   130
phone-checking behaviors   164
physical damage   112
poetry   4, 63, 69, 81–2, 188–9, 227–9
positive psychology   188
prayers   179
predicament   19
predictive coding   72
Proctor, John   187
prosocial behaviors   5, 72–3, 156
psychedelics   148
psychic predictions   70
psychological damage   112
Psychology Today   64–5, 70, 82
psychotherapy   116, 123
PTSD symptoms   30, 44, 72, 192
purpose
   awe and   72–3
   belonging and   4–5
   sense of   93

racing thoughts   44
racism   146
reassurance and love   170
recovery   114, 132
   model   51
   -oriented care   51
   process   134–5

red-tailed hawks   61, 191–7
Red Zinger tea   27
rehabilitation counseling   51–2
relational/cultural model of therapy   53
religion   177
resilience   139, 165, 168, *see also* wonder
   awe as a source of   80–2
   -building activities   106
   coping mechanism for trauma   67
   pathway 1: grounding, mindfulness, equanimity   200–1
   pathway 2: acceptance, peace of mind, serenity   201–2
   pathway 3: meaning and hope   202–3
   pathway 4: new perspectives, openness, "beginner's mind"   203–4
   pathway 5: connection, being part of something greater   204–6
   source of   3
   well-being and   74
reverence   8, 193
Richardson, Jan   179
right timing   105
Ross, Elizabeth Kubler   105
Rumi   40, 189
ruminations   44, 52, 73

SADOD (Support After a Death by Overdose)   86, 135–6
safety   16
SAMHSA (Substance Abuse and Mental Health Services Administration)   51
sanctuaries for healing in nature   36–7, 43, 62

satisfaction in work   26
schizophrenia   147–9, 151, 154
Schmaltz, Luke   111–26
science museums   175–6
screen time   121
scrolling   164–5, 192
self-absorption   71–2
self-assessment tool   74
self-care   151
self-centeredness   206
self-diminishment   75
self-discipline   164
self-improvement   140–1
self-loathing   52
self-mutilating behaviors   148, 154
self-referential thinking   71–3, 75, 154–5, 177
self-sacrificing heroes   16
self-transcendental emotions   71, 141, 156, 183–4, 203, *see also* awe
The Sense of Wonder   68, 165–6
serenity   62, 201–2
Seven Wonders of the World   176
sexual abuse   112, 123, 198
shame   139, 154, 156
   awkwardness and   42
sheer awe   119
shelter and safety   19
Shinto   178
Shiota, Michelle   72, 205
shoshin   203–4
Shriver, Maria   198
Sikhism   178
Silent Spring   2, 68
small self   71, 75
SNAP (Survivors Network of Those Abused by Priests)   115–16, 120, 122–3
social action event   170
social behavior   121

social judgment   121, 139
social life   63
social media   164–5, *see also* scrolling
social pressure   141–2
societal biases   70–1
soft light   14
solitude and relationships   38–9
soul gazing   182
spiritual/spirituality   12, 15–16, 176–83, 223–5
  awe   177
  bypassing   15–16
  connotation   97
  definition   178
  experiences   119
  growth   52
  hunger   12
  inspiring words and phrases   180
  religion and   176–83, 223–5
  signs and synchronicities   180–1
star gazing   182
St. Columba of Scotland   8
Stellar, Jennifer   72–3
stillness   25
Stolen Focus   192
story of awe   99
storytelling project   82, 85–6
strengths   49–53, 67, 69
  -based approach   49–52
  well-being and   199
stress   146
  anxiety and   197
  reducers   164
substance use disorder   90, 140, 151, 154
  prevention initiatives   132
suicidal thoughts   20
sun gazing   182
Sun Will Rise Foundation   3–4, 81, 86, 89, 133–4, 136

Support After Death by Overdose (SADOD)   86, 116–18
survivor of trauma   5
suspense and survival mode   99
Swart, Tara   181
synchronicities and signs   119, 135, 180

talk shows, interviews on   169
Taoism   178
tarot reader   17–18
terminal lucidity   184–5
Thompson, Derek   121
3-D IMAX films   175–6, *see also* museums
time/timing   24–5
  alterations in   75
  art of   2, 24–5
  -lapse cinematography   176
togetherness   98
totemism   183
toxins, cleansing and releasing   41–2
trauma
  and adversity, memoirs of   168, 216
  heal through wonder   141
  -informed care   33, 51
  and lack of knowledge   32–3, 51
  and loss   4, 40
  recovery   117
  survivors, benefits for   73–4, 107
  and treatment   33, 51
traumatized brain   44
tricks of light   16–20
trust and connection   53

ugliness to beauty   118
underappreciated emotions of awe and wonder   70
Unfixed Media   153

The Unfixed Mind series   152–3
unpredictability   67–8

Valjean, Jean   187
vastness   71, 75
Verywell Mind   177
victims of abuse   32–3, *see also* sexual abuse
violence   164, *see also* domestic violence
Virginia Commonwealth University   51
virtual tours   176, 223
visual awe   222–3
visual design (sacred geometries)   175–6
volatility   59
vulnerabilities   59, 127, 133

well-being   5, 72, 74, 78, 199
A White Heron   8
Williams, Terry Tempest   5
Williamson, Jennifer   179
willingness to be wondrous   197–9
Wolfe's Neck Woods State Park, Maine   57, 61, 66, 201
wonder   157, *see also* awe
  activity guides to inspire   212–13
  break   164
  chasers   102
  connection and   82
  definitions   71
  healing through sharing, and awe   127–42
  of life   77–8
  live with uncertainty   99–106
  for living   124
  realities and   68
  -seeking nature   70
  sense of   2–3, 7, 68
  sharing, in relationships and groups   95–9
  sharing moments of, with others   80–3
  as a source of strength   3
  for trauma survivors   3
  underappreciated emotions of   70
  of voice   115–20
  walks   164, 172
  websites to inspire wonder activities and expand our curiosity   213
wonderment   22, 120
Wordsworth, William   189, 229
World Atlas   177–8
worlds and domains of wonder   166
worlds of wonder   166–7
worship   177

Yaden, David   71
yelling   114
youthful sense of wonder   101

Zephyrus   11–12

ABOUT THE AUTHOR

Val Walker is a rehabilitation consultant, educator, and a contributing blogger for *Psychology Today* and the *Health Story Collaborative*. She is the author of *The Art of Comforting*, a Nautilus Book Award Gold Winner that was recommended by the Boston Public Health Commission as a guide for families impacted by the Boston Marathon bombing. She is also the author of *400 Friends and No One to Call* and speaks nationwide on building community and support after loss and major life changes. She has a Master of Science degree in rehabilitation counseling from Virginia Commonwealth University and has led support groups for twenty-five years for people living with illness, grief, and trauma. Based in Boston, she hosts storytelling events and facilitates workshops for recovery and grief support organizations, healthcare centers, and Councils on Aging centers. Catch up with Val at ValWalkerAuthor.com and learn more about healing through awe and wonder at HealingThroughWonder.com.